**7 DAY
BOOK**

Josef Marx/Günter Wagner

FIELD HOCKEY TRAINING
for Young Players

Meyer & Meyer Sport

Original title:
Hockeytraining – Spielgemäße Einführung
2., überarbeitete Neuauflage – Aachen: Meyer und Meyer Verlag, 2000

British Library Cataloguing in Publication Data
A catalogue for this book is available from the British Library

Marx/Wagner:
Field Hockey Training / Josef Marx ; Günter Wagner.
2nd Ed. – Oxford : Meyer & Meyer Sport (UK) Ltd., 2004
ISBN 1-84126-136-X

© 2001 by Meyer & Meyer Sport (UK) Ltd.
Aachen, Adelaide, Auckland, Budapest, Graz, Johannesburg,
Miami, Olten (CH), Oxford, Singapore, Toronto
Member of the World
Sports Publishers' Association (WSPA)
www.w-s-p-a.org
Printed and bound by: FINIDR, s. r. o., Český Těšín
ISBN 1-84126-136-X
E-Mail: verlag@m-m-sports.com
www.m-m-sports.com

Contents

Contents

Foreword by the Authors

In Germany we found that there was generally a reluctance in schools to include Hockey in the sports curriculum. We put this down to a lack of experience by the sports teachers in earlier years and also during their studies. However, following the successes of the German National Hockey team over recent years, hockey has gained more interest in Germany, and thus we decided to write a book, which would hopefully dispel some of the prejudices about the game, found principally in German schools. In the book we have provided training exercises for five game situations that show the correct way to play. Starting point is the simple thought of scoring a goal or preventing a goal being scored. In this way one begins to play hockey from the word go.

Our own experience, stretching back over several years, created the basis on which this book has been written. The connection between theory and practice has thus been optimised.

We are therefore particularly pleased to be able to have this book published in the English language. There is probably no doubt that Hockey in English speaking countries enjoys a greater popularity in youth circles than in Germany. Nevertheless, world-wide, it does have to compete with football and other goal scoring oriented sports. However, as a 'non-contact' game hockey is very suitable for boys and girls alike, and gives them a variety of fun and experience. This revised edition of the book is designed in the first instance for trainers and coaches — even those without any experience of hockey — students, exercise leaders and club trainers in the school and youth sectors.

Playing the game is always taken as the central point for discussion and is complemented by a large selection of game and exercise forms, tips about tactics, precise descriptions regarding movement and actions, correcting faults as well as a successive build up of the rules of the game.

At this juncture we would like to thank the German Hockey Union, in particular Mr Wolfgang Hillmann, for their friendly support. In addition thanks goes to Mr Horst Mevissen for the photographic work, Mr Lutz Thiesen for his advice regarding the technicalities of printing as well as to Mrs Hilde Marx for her untiring efforts on the typewriter.

Josef Marx   *Günter Wagner*

Foreword to the 1st (German Language) Edition

The development of hockey in recent years has taken an enormous upsurge and is enjoying a growing wave of popularity from the up and coming youth.

Hockey is continuously becoming popular in schools and with young people in clubs, and therefore there is a real necessity for a helpful reference book for use by the teachers in these establishments – principally designed for the inexperienced – in putting together the programme for teaching and training sessions.

In this book one can recognise the synergy between theory and practice. In this way the authors have placed a concept of actually playing the game to the fore, which gives those learning the game the opportunity to play from the very beginning.

The novel approach adopted in the book offers an interesting aspect, using simple means with a broad variation of motivating exercises.

The German Hockey Union recommends this book especially for use in schools and clubs.

Wolfgang Hillmann

Foreword

Following the successes of the German National Hockey Team, the German Hockey Union intensively seeks to further the cause of introducing the sport of hockey by employing expert children's and youth training in clubs and in schools.

A comprehensive text book about hockey for schools' sports teachers and coaches in the youth sectors of clubs, with genuine game forms is a particularly important adjunct and very welcome.

This book gives a good mixture of exercise and game forms for direct practical use.

It gives sports teachers, who lack experience of the game, the ability to construct a varied training programme, and gives coaches in the youth sector motivation for their training sessions.

I can thoroughly recommend this book.

Bernhard Peters
(former National Coach of the German Hockey Union)

Notes

Following the wider interest being shown in recent years for hockey as an alternative goal scoring game in school and leisure sports circles, it occurred to us that it would be the right time to supplement this development with a text book, which not only would give support to those playing the game, but also would be used to further the new didactic and methodical approach to the game.

Target Group

First of all, the target group of this book is teachers – particularly those with no experience in playing hockey – sports students, exercise instructors and club trainers of youth sections.

Didactic and methodical approach

The concept of this book has been based on the latest methods of teaching sports and games – allowing the beginner to learn by playing, acceptance of a child's ability to learn and the development of behavioural play, clear lesson planning, corrective training, avoidance of failure and loss of motivation, and the instilment and desire to take up the sport for life.

It all stems from the simplest of thoughts on the game, namely the idea of competing with the opponent for the ball with the aim of scoring a goal or preventing one being scored. Based on this principle, a concept of building up towards the actual game was conceived and developed in which the expansion of the basic form is built on until the complex form is reached. This leads to five game situations during which the beginner is taken from the simplest of game forms through to actually playing the game. In this way the player gets to learn about the continually changing situations of attacking and defending right from the beginning i.e., **he is already playing hockey!**

In order to be able to fit the various game situations together to be competent to play hockey, training is necessary to give experience so that technical skills and the tactical elements gradually and successively become ingrained. This applies also to the application of the rules on top of the basic principles.

Notes and how to use the book

The book is divided into 5 game situations:

1. Shooting a goal – preventing a goal
2. Scoring a goal by running and passing – preventing a goal by using the Sweeper
3. Working out goal scoring situations – preventing goals
4. Building up the game – closing down the game
5. Correct play – attacking/defending

Each game situation is divided into various frames:

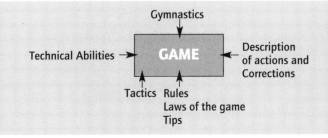

The central unit of each frame illustrates the play. The technical ability orientates itself around this, and is learned by using exercises and play sessions. These sessions can be selected at random and do not necessarily have to be slavishly followed in the particular order shown. In the same way tactical deliberations as well as the continuous build up of the list of rules, laws and tips can be added to gradually. The descriptions of the actions and movements are complemented with illustrations which bring additional clarity to the words, and assist the reader to be able to analyse these movements, put them into practice accurately and assist him in teaching them. The concluding corrective actions of common mistakes are given in detail, point by point, with the aim of preventing them happening in the first place.

The leading section for gymnastics has been constructed as forms for individual, partner assisted and as group exercises – with and without the hockey stick. Amongst other things these serve to prepare the body for the functional demands experienced in the game.

The gymnastics sections are not tied to any of the particular game situations and can be used in any of them.

The sports teacher is afforded a large variety of ways of planning and putting his training programme together so that he can make best use of available space, equipment and type of group being taught.

He will be able to combine the exercise and game forms into a given game situation.

Legend

Player	△ ◻ ○ ⓦ
Goalie	Ⓖ
Ball direction	- - - - - - - - -▶
Direction of the player without the ball	——————▶
Direction of the player with the ball	〜〜〜▶
Stopping the ball	〜〜⋏▶
Selling/giving a dummy (feinting)	〜〜〜▶
Supporting defenders	〜〜〜◢
Flicked/Aerial ball	〜〜〜▶
Shot at goal	══════▶
Player numbers	⚠ ⚠ ⚠
Consecutive route of player	▷—▶▷—▶▷
Consecutive route of ball	- - -▷- - -▷ ══▶
Connecting line	✕—✕—✕—✕—✕—✕—

Legend

Hockey ball	•
Hockey stick	J
Goal	
Shooting circle (also called the 'D')	
Open goal-mouth	P P
Flag poles	
Skittle	
Club	
Little box	
Large box	
Long bench	
Boards	
Base	
Gymnastic ring/tyre	O
Ball	
Full Pitch/Mini Hockey (Short Pitch)/Indoor Gymnasium	**FP/MH/I**
Forehand	**FH**
Reverse stick (Backhand)	**RS**

1. Gymnastics

1.1 Gymnastics with the Hockey Stick

1. Normal position

Side-step jump over the stick alternately from right to left and then from left to right.

2. Straddle standing

Holding the stick in both hands low down behind the back, lift the stick up from the rear as far as possible.

3. Straddle sitting

Hold the stick in both hands up in the air and slowly lie back. Lift the body back up quickly into the normal position.

4. Straddle standing

Swing the body sideways to the left and the right (springing the body at the top of the movement).

14

5. Sitting stretch

Squat on the ground and stretch the legs forward.

6. Lying in prone position

Lift the stick up gently. The nose almost touching the ground.

7. Sitting cross-legged

Swing the hips to the left and the right (bouncing the body at the end of the movement).

8. Kneeling in the straddled position

Lower the bottom slowly backwards, then – with the stick held up over the head – bend slowly forwards.

15

9. Sitting straddled

Slowly lift the hips up and lower them down again.

10. Sitting with outstretched leg

With the leg stretched out as far as possible from the bottom, swing the body in all directions holding the stick well out to the front.

11. Normal position

Alternately, left then right, swing the leg up forwards so that the instep touches the stick gently.

12. Sideways press-up

The stick is placed on the ground by the side of the player. With the free hand pick up the stick and lay it down on the other side.

13. Standing

Jump over the stick – left to right alternately (don't bend the knees too far).

14. Standing with straddled legs

Take your hand off the stick and spin round on your own axis; place the hand back on the stick.

15. Kneeling

Springing the body push the stick out further to the left and then lay it down on the right side.

16. Lying in supine position

Balancing the stick between your legs, pull the legs back over your head and then forward again to lay it on the ground.

17

1.2 Stretching Exercises

1. Step position

Position yourself with a long stride, legs apart – stretch the rear leg out as far as you can and stretch your hips up and down.

2. Knee press-up

Pull the upper body back. Fingers pointing backwards.

3. Normal position

Bend your arm up and push your left or right hand with the other one backwards and sideways as far as possible.

4. Straddle position

Touch the left ankle with the right hand and vice versa alternately.

5. Normal position

Holding on to the ankle, pull your leg up backwards against your bottom.

6. Normal position

Bend your arm and push it behind your head, simultaneously bending your body to the side.

7. Lying in supine position

Pull the head upwards and forwards with your hands until you can feel the strain.

8. Lying in prone position

Grasp your feet with your hands and slowly pull them onto your bottom.

9. Sitting stretch

Push down your legs which are pulled to your body.

10. Lying in supine position

Pull the bent knees against your body (head on the chest).

11. Sitting on the heels

Knees are together, the insteps on the ground; the heels are touching each other.

12. Crouching

Stretch the left leg out; the left hand presses the knee downwards; hand and legs alternately.

13. Step forward straddled

Push the leg out holding on to the knee and pressing against the joint; the hands support the stretching.

14. Sitting crossed leg

Press the legs out wide; the arms are stretched well upwards with open palms.

15. Lying in supine position

The legs lie stretched out on the ground; the bent leg is grasped with the hands below the knee and stretched.

16. Normal position

The legs are extended; the upper body is bent forward from the hips and the hands are laid on the hockey stick; upper body is pressed downwards.

21

17. Straddle position

Bend the upper body down deeply.

18. Normal position

Touch the wall with outstretched hand; body turns sideways.

19. Normal position

One arm supports the hip; the hand of the other arm grasps the head and pulls it to one side.

20. Squatting position

Bend the upper body forward, let the knees fall outwards.

21. Crouching

Crouching down press the knees outwards
with the upper arms.

22. Normal position

Fold the arms behind the back, bend the
upper body and stretch the arms.

23. Lying in supine position

Place the feet behind the head; press
through with the knees, stretch the arms.

24. Normal position

Stretch the left arm upwards, right hand
pulls the right foot up to the bottom; change
over sides.

23

1.3 Gymnastics with the Hockey Stick Using a Partner

1. Crouching

Half crouch down and hold onto the stick with arms outstretched.

2. Lying in supine position

Press-up on the partner's stick.

3. Kneeling

Step through over the partner's arms that are holding the stick without touching the partner's stick or his arms.

4. Lying in supine position

Slowly lift the knees up and down; knees should be slightly angled.

5. Lunging step

Alternately push the bottom backwards and forwards; additionally seesaw the stick on one side backwards and forwards; feet stay firmly placed.

6. Lunging step

Both partners push sharply against the stick.

7. Normal position

Player A holds the stick next to his shoulders; Player B stretches out the arms and pushes the stick away against the pressure of player A.

8. Lying in prone position

Holding the back straight, lift the upper body slightly off the ground and press the stick away against the pressure of the partner.

9. Sitting stretch

Both partners lift the left and right legs up high and press them out straddling the stick.

10. Normal position

Crawl through between the partner's arm and stick without touching them.

11. Normal position

Player A holds the stick out in front;
Player B jumps over the stick (on one leg or with both legs).

12. Sitting stretch

Bend the body forwards pulling the partner onto your back at the same time.

13. Crouching

Alternately the partners jump up and down; both partners jump up and down in unison (half crouch position).

14. Normal position

Throw the sticks to each other (using both hands: stick thrown horizontally/vertically – using one hand: stick thrown horizontally/vertically.

15. Kneeling

Bend the body to the left and then to the right.

16. Straddle sitting

Pull the partner gently forward.

1.4 Stretching Exercises with a Partner

1. Sitting on the heels

Widely straddled legs and simultaneous hip movements.

2. Normal position

Standing in the lunging position, turn the shoulders.

3. One behind the other

Stretching the shoulder standing one behind the other.

4. In twos

Lower and lift the upper body (shoulders and head).

5. Sitting on the heels

Controlled leaning back; partner ensures a
safe resistance.

6. Sideways straddle position

Bend to one side.

7. Lying in prone position

Partner joins the outstretched arms together.

8. Back to back

Back to back; join hands over the head; step
forward to do a bending movement.

9. Lying in supine position

With the upper body, carefully press forward against the raised legs of the partner lying down.

10. In twos

With arms crossed over do a sawing movement backwards and forwards.

11. Sitting stretch

The partner pulls the elbows and upper arms backwards as far as possible.

12. Forming a back

Pressing the shoulders against the resistance of the partner.

13. Normal position

Lift the leg up; partner gently presses the leg upwards.

14. Sitting position

Supporting the partner's back with the leg and slowly lift the arms upwards and backwards to stretch them.

15. Side straddle position

Grasp each other's hands and swing them up into the air sideways.

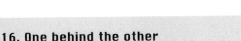

16. One behind the other

Slowly transfer the centre of balance onto the bent forward knee and pull the head back. Push the chest out as far as possible to the front.

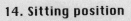

17. Normal position

Hold each other's leg up around the ankle; hop around in a circle.

18. In twos

Alternately pull up the upper body.

19. Back to back

Twist the upper body to the left and the right.

20. Standing straddled and angled

Turn the bottom to the left and the right.

21. Normal position

Lift the leg up to the left/right; swing the
leg freely.

22. Lying in prone position

Controlled pressing of the ankles against the
bottom.

23. Standing straddled
and angled

Whip the upper body up and down keeping
the back stiff.

24. Normal position

Hook the arms into each other and bend to
the left and the right.

1.5 Group Gymnastics with the Hockey Stick

1. Moving forward on all fours

Go on all fours scrabbling over the hockey sticks.

2. Moving backwards on all fours

In the reverse all fours position move over the sticks backwards.

3. Hopping

Hop over the sticks in a half crouched position.

4. Running

The sticks are strewn around the pitch – run backwards avoiding contact with the sticks.

5. Running

Run round outside the line of sticks; increase speed; change direction.

6. Running

Do a slalom down the line of sticks; increase speed; change direction.

7. Weaving

Do a slalom through the line of sticks weaving around the sticks (always run in the direction of the front stick).

8. Running

Run forward over the sticks; only one step allowed between the sticks.

35

9. Side gallop

Gallop over the sticks; change over the leading side of the body.

10. Skipping

Skip over sticks.

11. Hopping

Hop on one leg over the sticks, alternately left/right leg.

12. Hopping

Hop using both legs over the stick; swing the arms forwards and backwards.

13. Jumping

Jump forwards/backwards; jump sideways to the left/right; do a sword dance over the sticks.

14. Jump sideways

Jump sideways to the left/right over the line of sticks.

15. Hashing a stick

The sticks are strewn around the pitch with one less stick than players; on a command touch the sticks (go backwards on all fours as shown in picture).

16. Running

Catching your shadow.

17. Sitting stretch

Pairs lying down opposite each other; lift up the bottom whilst lying on the back, or lift body upwards and forwards; all together in unison or alternately.

18. Hashing in pairs

Two people grasp the stick together with their inside hands and try to cut another pair off.

19. Hurdling

Kneeling down, hold the stick at waist height; the players holding the sticks kneel about 1m away from each other; the hurdler creeps through the sticks , runs over the sticks or does consecutive one-legged jumps or two-footed jumps over them.

20. Climbing

Climb through a horizontal window.

2 Game Situations
2.1 Game Situation 1: Shooting a Goal – Preventing a Goal

2.1.1 Goal Shooting (Push Shot)

1. The game

The playing area is divided into two equal halves (about 5m each) and the group is divided into two equal strength sides. Starting from their own goal line, each side tries to push the ball over the opponent's goal line. When the ball crosses the line, or touches the wall, this counts as a goal. Foot faults and stick faults also count as goals.

2. Tactics

a) Attack

Try to get a goal by pushing the ball over the opponent's goal line. Push the ball fiercely into the opponent's half. Look carefully at the defence line-up.

b) Defence

Try to stop a goal being scored. Spread out along your own goal line to defend it. Watch the attacker carefully as soon as he begins his push.

3. Techniques

Forehand push shot

1. Shoot at the wall/an upturned bench/small boxes/large boxes.
2. Shoot into a confined area (marked out with skittles/medicine balls/marker flags/small boxes).
3. Aiming at small boxes/skittles/balls.

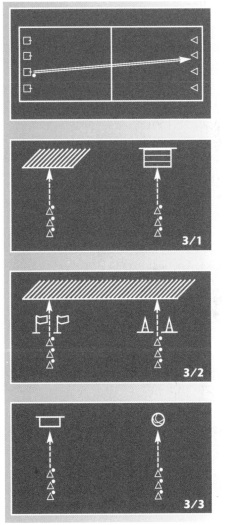

4. Skittles

Players are divided up into equal sized groups. Arrange the skittles/cones/balls etc., placing them in groups approximately 8-10 metres apart. Just as in skittles the aim is to knock the standing objects down by shooting at them. *Which team knocked them all down first?*

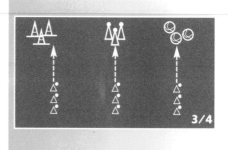

5. Skittle shooting

Two teams stand opposing each other. In the centre there are 6 yellow and 6 red skittles – one colour for each team. On the command each team tries to hit the opposing team's skittles by using the forehand push shot. *Each time a skittle is hit a point is scored.*

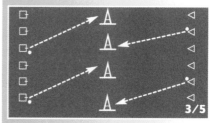

6. Moving the ball

Two teams stand opposing each other. At the beginning of each game a ball is placed in the middle between them. On the command each team tries to shoot at the ball to hit it. *Which team manages to move the ball nearest to the opposing team?*

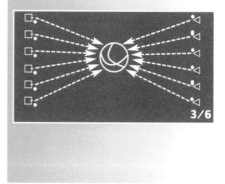

4. Description of the movements

Forehand push pass

1. The left shoulder is pointing in the direction of the pass.
2. The feet are positioned, slightly straddled shoulder-width; the line of the feet is pointing in the direction of the pass.
3. The knees are bent slightly.
4. The left hand grips the top of the stick.
5. The left hand is placed in the turn position; the 'V' (formed by the forefinger and thumb) running along the front edge of the stick.
6. The right hand is positioned about 2 hand-widths below the left hand on the grip binding.
7. The back of the right hand points in the opposite direction to the push pass.
8. The left lower arm forms an approximate straight line with the stick.
9. The wrist joints are held loosely.
10. The stick is angled at about 45° to the ground and between the legs at about 1-1 1/2 lengths of the foot away.
11. The head of the stick points upwards.
12. The head of the stick is directly behind the ball and is vertical to the ground.
13. At the start of the movement, the right shoulder is lower than the left for a fraction of a second.
14. When the stick is pulled back there is a short change of the centre of balance onto the rear (right) leg.
15. The push movement occurs by quickly pushing the right hand forward; the right hand comes forward of the left one.
16. A gentle pressure is applied by the left hand on the top of the stick.

17. The ball leaves the stick off the left foot.
18. The stick is carried forward level in the follow through (pointing at what you are aiming at).
19. The head of the stick points upwards.
20. Do not carry the stick up over shoulder height.

5. Incorrect movements

Forehand push pass

1. The stick is too near to the body.
2. The right hand grasps the stick too closely under the left hand.
3. The right hand, instead of the left hand, holds the top of the stick.
4. The ball is hit instead of being pushed.
5. The stick is played in a circling motion.
6. The stick is raised above shoulder height.
7. Holding the stick too short/wrong push direction.

6. Corrective measures

Forehand push pass

1. Place the head of the stick about 1 1/2 feet in front of the body.
2. Increase the distance between the hands to approximately 2 hand-widths.
3. Changeover the hands
4. Place the head of the stick directly behind the ball; bring the head of the stick just above the ground; avoid the stick impacting with the ball; the partner places his foot behind the head of the stick.
5. Bring the head of the stick over a straight line marked on the ground.
6. Brake the motion of the stick in the follow through.
7. Carry the head of the stick for longer behind the ball.

7. The rules

1. You can only take part in the game if you are carrying a stick. (FP/MH/I)
2. Only play the ball with the flat side of the head of the stick. (FP/MH/I)
3. The ball should roll along the ground in the push pass. (FP/MH/I)
4. You cannot strike the ball when pulling the stick back. (I)
5. Do not follow-through over shoulder height (dangerous play). (FP/MH/I)
6. Don't touch the ball with the foot or the leg (foot fault). (FP/MH/I)

8. The laws

The stick

The stick must possess a flat edge on its left side. The flat side includes the head of the stick and the whole length of the shaft (including grip binding). The head of the stick must be made from wood; it must have smoothed edges. The weight of the stick must not be more than 737 grammes. The stick must be able to be passed through a 5.10 cm ring. There are no regulations concerning length. The recommended length for a student is 36 ins.

2.1.2 Three Area Exercise

1. The game

The play area is divided into three equal areas; the three teams are of equal size. Each team occupies one of the three areas. The teams in the outside areas try to push the ball to each other. The team in the middle area try to prevent the passes. Stopped balls are passed on to the team in the opposing end. Each stopped ball scores a point. Foot and stick faults score minus points. Each team plays once in the middle area. The winner is the team that scores the most stopped ball points in a particular time.

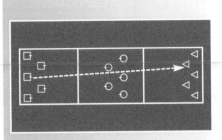

2. Tactics

a) Attack

Having gained ball control – play on. Push the ball hard and fast into the opposing area. Push through the holes in the opposing team's defence.

b) Defence

Try to stop the ball dead and under control. Change your positioning so that you can stop the ball with the forehand side. Cover the gaps. Defend your own goal line.

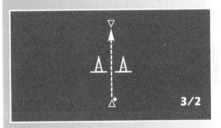

3/1

3. Techniques

Forehand push pass – stopping the ball forehand

1. Gentle forehand push pass to partner who stops the ball.
2. Push pass to partner in a confined space (through skittles/balls/marker flags/jumping rope/stands).
3. Push pass to a partner and then run up to a new position in a three or four area group.

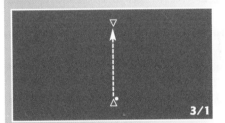

3/2

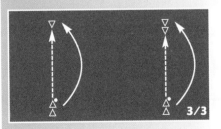

3/3

4. Pyramid relay:

The players stand (as illustrated) in a line. The 'server', standing in front of the group, pushes the ball to the players in turn. Each player pushes the ball back to the server. When the last person in the line receives the ball the No1 player changes places with the server. The game carries on until all the players have been the server. *Which group completes the series first?*

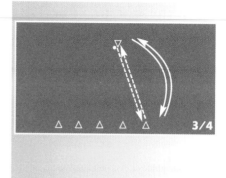

5. Basic lane relay

The group forms up on each side of a lane. The ball is passed from one to the other across and down the lane until it reaches the last player. If there are sufficient balls additional balls can be introduced into the lane (and also be passed back up the lane). *Which team succeeds in passing the ball(s) all through first?*

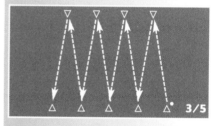

6. Passing the ball in the circle

The group forms a circle. One player stands in the centre of the circle. The players in the circle pass the ball to the player in the middle, who immediately passes it on to the next player in the circle. *Which team completes 1..2..3.. rounds first?*

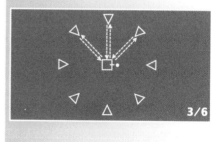

4. Description of the movements

Forehand stopping

1. The left shoulder points in the direction of the pass.

2. The feet are positioned, slightly more than shoulder-width apart, pointing in the direction from which the pass is coming.

3. The knees are bent slightly.

4. The left hand grips the top of the stick.

5. The left hand is placed in the turn position.

6. The right hand is positioned about 2 hand-widths below the left hand on the grip binding.

7. The back of the right hand points in the opposite direction from which the pass is coming.

8. The left lower arm forms an approximate straight line with the stick.

9. The wrist joints are held loosely.

10. The stick is angled at about 45° to the ground and between the legs at about 1-1 1/2 lengths of the foot away.

11. The right shoulder is lower than the left one.

12. Take the ball between the feet; head over the ball.

13. Bring the stick back to slow the ball down.

14. Change of the centre of balance onto the rear (right) leg.

15. Bring the ball under control for the return push pass.

5. Incorrect movements

Forehand stopping

1. The ball runs under the head of the stick.
2. The ball jumps or runs over the head of the stick; watch for incorrect stick angle.
3. The ball bounces off the stick.
4. The toe of the stick is held crooked to the direction of the pass; the ball runs in front of the feet or off to one side into the playing area.
5. The ball bounces off the head of the stick back into the playing area; no ball control.

6. Corrective measures

Forehand stopping

1. Make sure the head of the stick is on the ground.
2. Take up the correct stick position over the ball; press the left hand harder against the incoming ball.
3. Try to avoid impacting the stick on the ball as it arrives at the head of the stick; pull the head slightly back as it arrives.
4. Keep the head of the stick correctly placed for the direction of the incoming ball.

7. The rules

1. Only stop the ball with the flat side of the stick (stick fault). (FP/MH/I)
2. You may not stop the ball with the hand or catch it. (FP/MH/I)
3. If, later, you are a goalkeeper, other rules apply. (FP/MH/I)

8. The laws

The ball

The ball must be hard and round. It is made of natural or synthetic material.

Hockey, these days is normally played on an asphalt or synthetic pitch and the ball is seamless. For hockey played on grass, the ball can have a seam, but can also be seamless. It will normally be white or any other agreed colour.

For indoor hockey the ball must not have a seam, and it must be a different and distinct colour to the floor; usually a yellow or orange artificial ball.

The weight of the ball may not exceed 156 grammes nor be less than 163 grammes. The circumference of the ball may not be larger than 23.5 cm and not less than 22.4 cm.

2.1.3 From Midfield

1. The game

The playing area is divided into two equal sized areas. The teams pass the ball amongst themselves in their own half. They try to push the ball over the opponent's goal line from the midfield position to score a point. Hitting the wall also scores a point.

2. Tactics

a) Attack

Take up your position as required. Don't wait for the ball. Break away from the defence and run towards the ball. By running off the ball you create space for a good attacking position. If one of your team has a better position, pass the ball on as soon as you have ball control. You can also pass from the reverse stick side.

b) Defence

Position yourself together with your team so that you cover the whole of the goal line. Cover all the gaps. Change over positions within the team.

3. Techniques

Reverse stick push pass – forehand stopping

1. Reverse stick pass to the partner who stops with forehand.
2. Reverse stick pass to the partner in a confined space.
3. Reverse stick pass to the partner along a straight line.

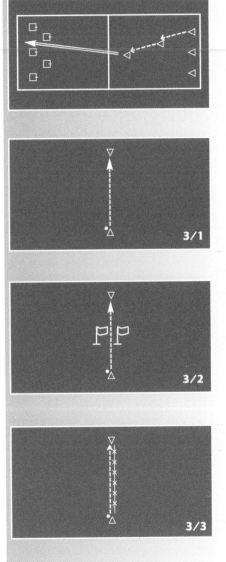

4. Along the row relay

The players stand, as illustrated, in a row. The first one plays the ball using the reverse stick to the 'server', who is standing in front. The server returns the ball to the second player also using the reverse stick. In the meanwhile the first player runs to the back of the row. After all have gone through the server is changed over. *Which team is the first to have all its players being the server?*

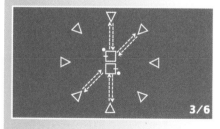

5. Passing the ball in the circle

The players form a circle. The ball is passed using the reverse stick to the next player in the circle. If a mistake is made the ball is brought back into play where the mistake occurred. *Which team completes 1..2..3.. rounds first?*

6. The chase game

The players form a circle. Two players stand in the centre of the circle with their backs to each other. On opposite sides of the circle two balls are brought into play – one on each side. The players in the circle pass the ball to the centre players who pass it straight away to another player in the outer circle. The centre players turn round as the ball moves round. *Which ball can be intercepted by the other centre player?*

48

4. Description of the movements

Reverse stick push pass

1. The left shoulder points in the direction of the pass.
2. The feet are positioned, slightly straddled, pointing in the direction of the pass.
3. The knees are bent slightly.
4. The left hand grips the top of the stick.
5. The left hand is placed in the turn position; the back of the hand is facing in the direction of the pass.
6. The toe of the stick points down to the ground.
7. The right hand is positioned about 2 hand-widths below the left hand on the grip binding.
8. The right hand points in the direction of the push pass (V form of the hand).
9. The left lower arm forms an approximate straight line with the stick.
10. The wrist joints are held loosely.

11. The stick is angled at about 45° to the ground.
12. The ball lies between the legs at about 1-1 1/2 feet away.
13. The flat side of the head of the stick is directly behind the ball and is vertical to the ground.
14. The right shoulder is lower than the left.
15. When the stick is pulled back there is a short change of the centre of balance onto the rear (left) leg.
16. The push movement occurs by quickly pushing the right hand forward.
17. A gentle pressure is applied by the left hand on the top of the stick.
18. The ball leaves the stick off the right foot.

19. The stick is carried through level (correct aiming).
20. Do not carry the stick up over shoulder height (foul play).

5. Incorrect movements
Reverse stick push pass

1. The left hand is not in the turn position.
2. The right hand is turning with the other hand.
3. The stick is angled too sharply; the ball is too close to the body.
4. The round side of the stick head was used.
5. The ball runs obliquely; the stick is being played in a circling motion.
6. The pass was not crisp enough.
7. The head of the stick was not pointing in the direction of the pass.
8. The stick was lifted over shoulder height.

6. Corrective measures
Reverse stick push pass

1. Turn the back of the hand more towards the ground; take a firmer grip of the binding.
2. Form a larger gap between hands.
3. Place the ball about 1 1/2 foot lengths away from the body.
4. The toe of the stick should point towards the ground.
5. Bring the head of the stick over a straight line marked on the ground.
6. Pull harder with the right hand.
7. Carry the head of the stick longer behind the ball.
8. Brake the motion of the stick in the follow through.

7. The rules

1. You are only allowed to play the ball with the flat side of the stick in the reverse stick push pass; touching the ball with the rounded sides of the head of the stick is considered as a foul. (FP/MH/I)
2. Kicking the ball, picking it up or carrying the ball is not allowed. (FP/MH/I)
3. You may not participate in play when lying on the ground. (I)

8. The laws
Clothing and equipment

The player may not have any dangerous appendages on the shoes, as well as have any equipment, which could endanger another player. It is now a rule that both outdoor and indoor hockey players must wear shin pads and knuckle protectors. For their own protection goalkeepers in youth teams must wear proper goalkeeping clothing. (For goalkeeping equipment see page 97).

2.1.4 Four Area Exercise

1. The game

The playing area is divided into four equal areas. Team No 1 and 3 play together just as teams 2 and 4 do. The aim is to pass the ball through the opposition to the other friendly team, or intercept it, and thus build up a team game together. Teams change round areas after a specified time. Which team has scored the most through passes or interceptions?

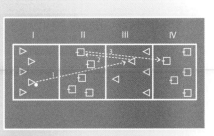

2. Tactics

a) Attack

Make use of the area and run to collect the ball. Play quickly to a team member or to the other area team members. Make use of the gaps occurring in the opposition and play the ball directly.

b) Defence

Also use the reverse stick to stop the ball; in this way you will play more rapidly and this places you in a better attacking position. Arrange yourself together with the other team members so that all the gaps are covered. Provide good cover for your team members.

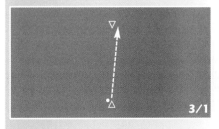

3/1

3. Techniques

Reverse stick push pass – reverse stick stop

1. Play a reverse stick push pass to a partner who stops the ball on the reverse stick.
2. Practice reverse stick push passes and reverse stick stopping within the team group with changeovers.
3. Play reverse stick push passes and reverse stick stopping followed up with a change of position.

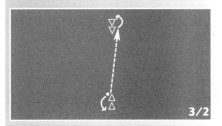

3/2

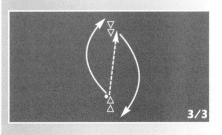

3/3

51

4. Playing the ball in a circle

The group stands in a circle. The ball is played to a player at random round the circle. The person who has passed the ball runs to the place where he has passed the ball and takes up that position in the circle. All the players in the circle receive the ball once in a round. *Which team has finished one (or more) round(s) first?*

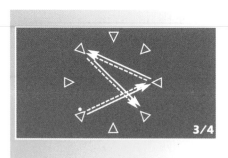

5. Chasing the ball in the lane

Two teams stand interspersed with each other at about 3m distance in a lane. The ball (one for each team) is passed diagonally to the next opposite friendly player. The aim is to attempt to overtake the other team's ball. Opponents' passes should not be intercepted. If there is an incorrect pass the game picks up again from where the fault was made. *Which team's ball is passed down the lane (and back again) first?*

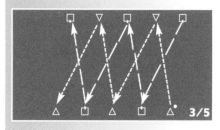

6. Corner ball with changing positions

The players stand in the four corners of a square. Two balls are brought into play on opposite sides of the square. The ball is passed anti-clockwise round the square to the next player. After playing the ball each player changes position to the diagonally opposite spot. *Which group completes 1, 2, 3 rounds first?*

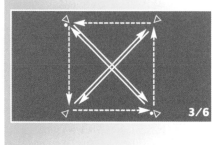

4. Description of the movements

a) Reverse stick stop

1. The right shoulder points in the direction of the pass.
2. The feet are positioned, slightly straddled, pointing in the direction of the incoming ball.
3. The knees are bent slightly.
4. The left hand grips the top of the stick.
5. The left hand is placed in the turn position; the head of the stick points to the ground; the back of the hand faces in the direction of the incoming ball.

6. The right hand is positioned about 2 hand-widths below the left hand on the grip binding, (forming an eyelet).
7. The back of the right hand points in the direction of the incoming ball.
8. The left lower arm forms an approximate straight line with the stick.
9. The wrist joints are held loosely.
10. The stick is angled at about 45° to the ground.

11. The toe of the stick points to the ground.
12. The ball lies between the legs at about 1-1 1/2 feet away; watch out for correct stick angle.
13. Pull the head of the stick back; slow down the speed of the ball.
14. Change the centre of balance onto the rear (left) leg.

15. Stop the ball dead; maintain ball control for an eventual return reverse stick push pass.

b) Reverse stick stop and run forward

1. The left shoulder points in the direction of the pass.

2. The right shoulder points in the direction of the incoming ball.

3. The feet are positioned slightly straddled; prepared to run in a forward direction.

4. The knees are bent slightly.

5. Glance over the right shoulder in the direction of the incoming ball.

6. The left hand grips the top of the stick.

7. The left hand is placed in the turn position; the toe of the stick points to the ground; the back of the hand faces in the direction of the incoming ball.

8. The right hand is positioned about 2 hand-widths below the left hand on the grip binding (forming an eyelet) .

9. The back of the right hand points in the direction of the incoming ball.

10. The left lower arm forms an approximate straight line with the stick.

11. The wrist joints are held loosely.

12. The stick is angled at about 45° to the ground.

13. The toe of the stick points to the ground.

14. The ball lies between the legs at about 1-11/2 feet away; watch out for correct stick angle to protect the ball.

15. Pull the head of the stick in the direction of the front foot; slow down the speed of the ball.

16. Change the centre of balance onto the front (left) leg.

17. Stop the ball dead; maintain ball control.

18. Turn the stick into the forehand position.

19. Bring the head of the stick behind the ball.

20. Take the ball with you as you run forward.

21. Look in the direction you are running.

5. Incorrect movements

a) Reverse stick stop

1. The ball is being stopped too early; the stick is being obliquely angled; the ball runs or jumps over the head of the stick.
2. The stick is too upright; the ball bounces off the stick.
3. Watch out for correct stick angle to protect the ball.
4. The head of the stick is oblique to the direction of the pass; the ball runs in front of the feet or sideways into the area.
5. The rounded side of the head of the stick plays the ball.
6. Wrong turn grip.
7. The right hand turns at the same time.

b) Reverse stick stop and run forward

1. The knees are not bent.
2. You are not looking backwards.
3. The stick is not being held in the reverse stick position.
4. The ball bounces off the stick; it is being stopped too abruptly.

6. Corrective measures

a) Reverse stick stop

1. Stop the ball later, level with the left foot; protect the ball by angling the stickhead more.
2. Correct your position on the ball; stop the ball to the side of your body.
3. Press your hand more in the direction of the incoming ball.
4. Place the head of the stick at right angles to the path of the ball.
5. The toe of the stick must point towards the ground.
6. Turn the back of the hand more towards the ground.
7. Form a larger gap between the hands on the stick.

b) Reverse stick stop and run forward

1. Bend the knees more.
2. Look in the direction of the incoming ball.
3. Turn the stick into the reverse stick position; the left hand points in the running direction; only stop the ball with the flat side.
4. Take the ball on a little more gently in order to slow it down; watch out for the correct stick angle and position to protect the ball.

7. The rules

1. Only use the flat side of the stick when doing the reverse stick stop. (FP/MH/I)
2. You may not use any part of the body to hold on to or deflect the ball – on the ground or in the air. (FP/MH)
3. For point 2 above there are other rules for the goalkeeper (see page 60/7.2 and page 141/7). (FP/MH/I)

8. The laws

Teams

A team consists of 11 players and 5 substitutes. (FP)

A team for mini-hockey consists of 6 players and 3 substitutes. (MH)

For indoor hockey the team consists of 6 players and 6 substitutes. (I)

For outdoor hockey each team may substitute 5 players during the game. (FP)

A player who has been already substituted may retake the field. (FP/MH/I)

Substitution can take place at any time except after the award of a penalty corner. Substitution takes place on the centre line, or another point on the side line agreed to by the umpires beforehand; players shake hands or tap the other's hand as they pass each other. (FP/MH)

Substitution is only allowed when the ball goes dead over the goal or the base line, or when a goal has been scored; prior to replay following a short corner when a goal has not been scored; when play restarts and during half-time. Injured players can be substituted at any time after consultation with the umpire.

Substitution can only be made in the region of the team benches. (I)

2.2 Game Situation 2 Scoring a Goal by Running and Passing - Preventing a Goal by Using the Sweeper

2.2.1 Moving up to the Goal Area

1. The game

The attacking game is played with a 2:1 attack majority against the sweeper in the goal area. The sweeper, using long stick tackles, stands in front of the defence who are protecting the goal line, and tries to prevent shots being taken at goal. The attack occurs in trying to separate the sweeper from the goal line defenders. During the attack a defender leaves the goal line, and together with the sweeper creates a majority. When the attack is over the attacker becomes the sweeper and the sweeper goes to the goal line. The changeover carries on until all players have been the sweeper at least once.

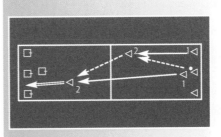

2. Tactics

a) Attack

Run to the outside position in order to nullify the sweeper's influence.

Using the reverse stick push shot, try to get round the gap in the defence.

Shoot (push shot) hard at the opponents goal area.

b) Defence

In order to avoid a goal, use the extended distance to your advantage; you don't have to run so far, and you can defend more effectively.

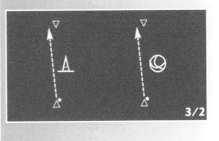

Position yourself in front of the defence so that you can intercept with a low forehand stick; the attacker will have to switch over early to play on the reverse stick.
Defend the goal line from various positions. If you manage to get the ball as the sweeper, you are automatically the foremost player in the attack.

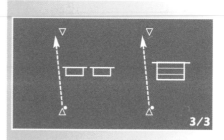

3. Techniques

Stopping with lowered body position / forehand

1. Diagonal pass to your partner who stops the ball with a low forehand stick.
2. Pass the ball past an obstacle (skittle, cone, ball) to your partner who stops the ball with a low forehand stick.
3. Diagonal pass past a larger obstacle (skipping rope, small boxes, large boxes (thus creating a larger optical difficulty)) to your partner who stops the ball with a low forehand stick.

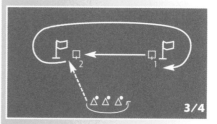

4. Chase the defender

A player standing between two marker flag poles positions himself at the left hand flag pole. From a distance of about 4 m the remaining players, standing in a line, push the ball towards the right hand flag pole one after the other. The player at the flag pole stops the ball with a low stick and then runs round the flag poles to where he started from. During this, the next player pushes the ball at the flag pole. *Who manages to stop the most balls?*

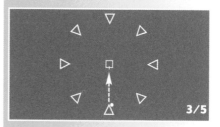

5. Tiger ball

The group stands in a circle with the "tiger" in the middle. The players pass the ball across the circle to each other (except you cannot pass

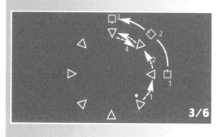

the ball to your neighbour). The tiger tries to intercept the ball using a low stick. If the tiger stops the ball he changes position with the last player to touch the ball. *Which tiger plays for the shortest period?*

6. Tease game
The group stands in a circle and plays the ball round circularly – the direction is not important. Outside the circle a player runs round and tries to intercept the ball using a low stick. If he succeeds in doing so he changes position with the last player to pass the ball. *Who manages to achieve an interception?*

4. Description of the movements

Stopping with lowered body position / forehand

1. Position is frontal towards the incoming ball.
2. The feet may be positioned between an open straddle stance to being closed.
3. Knees slightly bent.
4. The hands grasp the stick just like the forehand stop.
5. Let go of the stick with the right hand.
6. Bring the stick round in front of the body with the left hand.
7. Step over the right foot with the left foot.
8. Go into a crouched position.
9. Bring the stick parallel to the ground.
10. The flat side of the stick points in the direction of the incoming ball.
11. The stick and the ground form a triangle; the toe of the stick points upwards **(angled to protect the ball)**.
12. If possible stop the ball dead; gain ball control for the subsequent push pass.

5. Incorrect movements

*Stopping with lowered body position/
forehand*

1. The ball runs under the stick.
2. The ball runs or jumps over the head of the stick.
3. The stick is too upright; the ball bounces off the stick. Wrong protective stick angle and position.
4. The stopping surface is too small.
5. The ball runs along the stick to the hand.
6. No ball control gained to allow a further push pass onwards.
7. You don't reach the ball.

6. Corrective measures

*Stopping with lowered body position/
forehand*

1. Push the stick down parallel to the ground until the fingers are touching it.
2. Form a triangle between the head and the stick; turn the toe of the stick harder towards the direction of the incoming ball.
3. Bend the knees more.

4. Place the stick at right angles to the direction of the pass.
5. Stretch up quicker from the knees bend position into the standing position.
6. Over-emphasise the step over the right foot with the left foot.

7. The rules

1. When you stop the ball with the low stick, you may use the whole length of the stick. But here too, you are only allowed to use the flat side. (FP/MH/I)
2. Stopping the ball or catching it by the hand is not allowed (with the exception of the goalkeeper). However, it is not forbidden to protect yourself against a dangerous high ball with the hand. (FP/MH/I).

8. The laws

The layout of the indoor hockey pitch

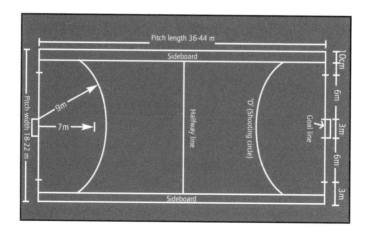

2.2.2 Attack on the Goal

1. The game

The game is played with a 2:1 attack majority using a 'neutral' player. The game is similar to 'Moving up to the goal area'. The neutral player is always the attacker so that the defence is always under pressure. The sweeper also plays as an attacker, and is changed over with one of the defenders after a specific period of time. The same applies to the neutral player (marked "N"). The defender should also use the reverse stick side to defend the goal.

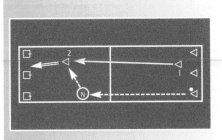

2. Tactics

a) Attack

The distance from the sweeper has increased; play faster against the 'neutral' player, while the sweeper cannot always position himself to the best. As the 'neutral' player you have to adapt constantly to a new partner situation, which demands flexibility. As the 'neutral' player take up the outside position thus enabling you to get round the sweeper.

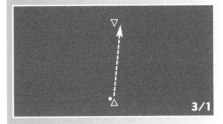

3/1

b) Defence

Stop the ball using both the open (forehand) and reverse stick side. By doing this you gain more control over a broader part of the pitch. As a sweeper do not be tempted out of the central defence position. Because a larger distance is created this is no longer necessary. If you win the ball you count automatically as an attacker. Goal line defenders move up into the position of the sweeper.

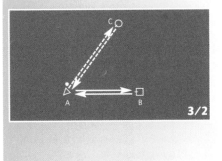

3/2

3. Techniques

*Stopping with lowered body position /
reverse stick side*

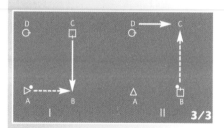

1. Pass diagonally to a partner, who stops it low on the reverse stick side.

2. Triangular changeover of places

Player A and B change positions. The player running towards position A stops the ball with a low reverse stick stop. Player C passes the ball to position A. Each player passes through each position.

3. Taking positions in a square

The ball is played towards the unoccupied corner of the square and another player has to chase after it to stop it using a low reverse stick stop. Players run round the square clockwise whilst the ball moves in an anti-clockwise direction.

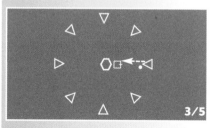

4. Chase the defender (Variation)

A player, standing between two marker flag poles, positions himself at the left hand flag pole. From a distance of about 4 metres the remaining players stand in a line. A server pushes the ball towards the first player in the line who pushes the ball further towards the right hand flag pole. The player at the flag pole stops the ball with a low reverse stick, stops, and then runs round the flag poles to where he started from. The server takes up his place at the end of the row and the shooter becomes the server.

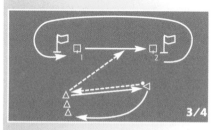

5. Target ball.

The players stand in a circle. In the middle there is a "target" erected (a ball for example), which is defended by a player. Players in the circle try to hit the target. The player managing to hit the target changes places with the defender. Who is the best at defending the target?

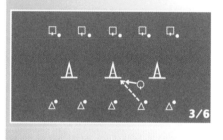

6. Defending skittles

Two groups stand in line opposite each other; skittles are placed on the ground between the groups and a player defends them. The groups alternately try to hit the skittles. The defender wards off attacks from both groups. After a specific time each group provides the defending player. *Which defender has the least hits scored against him?*

4. Description of the movements

Stopping with lowered body position / reverse hand

1. Position is frontal towards the incoming ball.
2. The feet may be positioned between an open straddle stance to being closed.
3. Knees slightly bent.
4. The hands grasp the stick just like the reverse stick stop.
5. Let go of the stick with the right hand.
6. Bring the stick round in front of the body with the left hand.
7. Step over the left foot with the right foot.

8. The left hand turns the stick into the reverse stick position so that the toe of the head is pointing towards and resting on the ground.
9. Go into a crouched position.
10. Bring the stick parallel to the ground – as far as possible.
11. Hold the flat side of the stick in the direction of the incoming ball.

12. Push the stick forward towards the ground so that the ball will not run under the arch formed by the stick head; form a triangle between the stick and the ground noting the correct stick angle and position (to protect the ball).
13. Stop the ball dead as far as possible; gain ball control for the subsequent push pass.

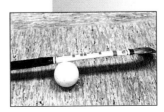

5. Incorrect movements

Stopping with lowered body position / reverse hand

1. The ball runs under the arch formed by the stick head.
2. The ball runs through under the stick head.
3. The ball is played with the rounded side of the stick.
4. The ball runs along the stick to the hand.
5. No ball control gained to allow a further push pass onwards.
6. You don't reach the ball.

6. Corrective measures

Stopping with lowered body position / reverse hand

1. Form a flatter protective stick angle position; push the stick out further towards the incoming ball; stop the ball more in the middle of the stick.
2. Bend the knees more; push the stick further down until the fingers are touching the ground.
3. The toe of the head must point towards the ground.
4. Place the stick at a right angle to the direction of the pass.
5. Stretch up quicker from the knees bend position into the standing position.
6. Over-emphasise the step over the right foot with the left foot; stretch the arm through further.

7. The rules

At the beginning of the first half, the second half and after a goal has been scored, the game is restarted only by using the push pass from the middle of the field. A restart in hockey is known as a "bully-off". You may only cross over the halfway line of the pitch after the ball has been played. At the start of play no other player may be nearer than 5 m to the ball. Apart from the person playing the ball, all the other players must stay in their own half. (FP/MH).

In the indoor game no opponent may be closer than 3 m to the ball. The player bullying-off may not stay in the vicinity, or approach, or play the ball again before another player has played the ball. (FP/MH/I).

8. The laws

Layout of the mini hockey pitch

A Official layout; goal posts as per normal pitch.

B Only permitted for local league competitions; goal posts as per handball.

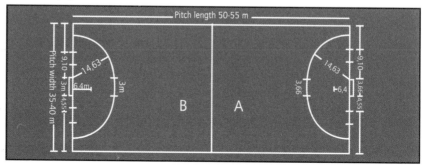

2.2.3 Exercising in Zones

1. The game

Played as an attack game with an attack majority of 3:2. The pitch is made up of two goal mouth areas and a central zone (strip). An oversize goal is marked out at each end using flag poles on each of the goal lines. The central zone can only be passed by using a forehand pass. Similarly goals can only be scored by using a forehand shot within the shooting circle. In order to maintain the majority the attacker (marked 'x') may not return to his own half. Everyone has to rotate through this position.

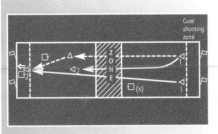

2. Tactics

a) Attack

Hit the ball in order to cover a long distance. Hit the ball hard when passing; thus it will be harder and more difficult to defend against these passes. Collect and quickly hit the ball into the oversized goal.

b) Defence

Tackle the attacker quickly in your own half since he can cover long distances with his hit. Also use the hit stroke; this way you can clear the ball quicker out of the danger zone. If you lose the ball, run immediately towards your goal. Switch back to a defensive position as soon as possible.

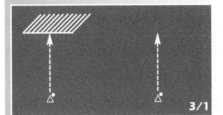

3/1

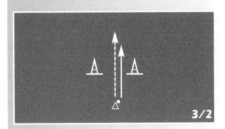

3/2

3. Techniques

Hitting a static ball forehand

1. Hit the ball against a wall; hit the ball into an empty area.
2. Hit the ball through skittles and follow up running (hitting accuracy).

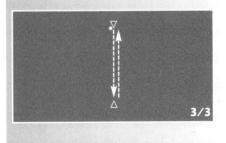

3/3

3. Hit the ball to a partner.

4. Hitting the ball through a skittle alley

Each team forms up in two rows behind each other. The ball is hit through the alleyway formed by the skittles to the team standing opposite. If the ball doesn't get through to the opposing player successfully it has to be gathered up into the playing area again. Each player runs, following up the ball, to a new position. *Which team manages to complete a session?*

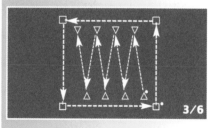

5. Rapid shooting at the goal

Members of a group, each in turn, shoot four to six balls in rapid succession at a goal made from poles. Afterwards each player takes up his position at the back of the team. *Which player achieves the most goals with a correct shot?*

6. The hare versus the tortoise

The ball is passed around four players (the hares) standing in each corner of a square. Eight players (the tortoises) are standing to form a lane inside the square and pass the ball amongst them as shown in the picture. Each player must chase after the ball he passes on, if it doesn't reach the next player (hares or tortoises). *Who finishes first; the hares or the tortoises?*

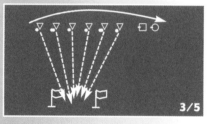

4. Description of the movements

Hitting a static ball – Forehand

1. The left shoulder points in the direction of the hit.
2. The feet are positioned in a broad straddled position at right angles to the direction of the hit.
3. The left hand firmly grasps the top of the stick with the back of the hand pointing in the direction of the hit.

4. The right hand grasps the stick directly under the left hand with the back of it pointing away from the direction of the hit.
5. The stick is angled at about 25° to the ground.
6. The ball lies between and at a distance of approximately 3/4 of the length of the stick in front of the feet.
7. The knees are bent slightly; body centre of balance held low.
8. The upper arms are pushed out slightly from the body.
9. The lower arms are stretched out.
10. The stick is pulled back no higher than hip height.
11. When pulled back the toe of the stick end points upwards and the flat side of the stick is held vertically to the ground.
12. The wrists and the right lower arm are angled more than the left arm.
13. Change the centre of balance onto the rear (right) leg.
14. As the ball is hit, the wrist and the arm joints are consciously stretched outwards.
15. The flat side of the stick head strikes the ball at the bottom of the swing; the toe of the stick end points away from the body.
16. As the ball is hit the centre of balance moves from the rear leg onto the forward leg.
17. The stick is followed through straight behind the ball.
18. Actively brake the stick in a flat swing movement; maximum height at hip level.
19. At the end of the swing, the toe of the stick end points upwards; the flat side of the stick is vertical to the ground.

5. Incorrect movements

Hitting a static ball – forehand

1. The toe of the stick end points away from the body.
2. You miss the ball, stick passing over it.
3. You hit the ground.
4. You hit (slice) the top of the ball.
5. The hands grasp the stick too far apart.
6. The left hand is not grasping the stick from the side.

7. The stick is lifted above hip height when pulling back.

8. The stick is lifted above hip height in the follow through phase.

9. The stick is lifted above shoulder height (considered dangerous play only if someone is close = foul play).

10. The ball runs away to the left and not in the desired direction.

11. Wrong centre of balance.

6. Corrective measures

Hitting a static ball – forehand

1. Turn the toe of the stick end up to "heaven"!

2. Get nearer to the ball.

3. Move further away from the ball.

4. Don't bend the arms so much; they should be stretched out as you hit the ball.

5. Push the hands further together at the top end of the stick.

6. Move the hand into the basic hold position; the back of the hand should point in the direction of the stroke.

7. Make sure the stick doesn't come above hip height.

8. Consciously control the stick at hip height.

9. Don't swing the stick above shoulder height (foul play).

10. Bring the stick straight down and not in an arched movement; run the stick along a straight line.

11. Consciously shift the centre of balance from the rear leg onto the forward leg.

7. The rules

1. You are allowed to stroke hit the ball in both full-pitch and mini-hockey. (FP/MH).

2. It is forbidden to strike the ball while it is in the air, when the strike action would be dangerous for other players. You are not allowed to flip the ball up and then strike it in the air with the stick. (FP/MH/I).

3. If you hit the ball into the air/off the ground, it is considered dangerous play if the opponent is forced to take avoiding action. (FP/MH/I).

8. The laws

Dimensions of the full size outdoor hockey pitch

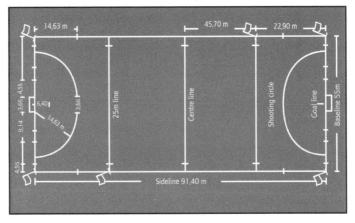

2.2.4 Exercising in Halves

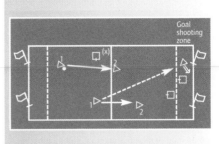

1. The game

The game is played with a 3:2 attack majority. Oversized goal mouths, marked out by using flag poles, are placed at each end on the goal line. The team in possession of the ball strikes the ball into the opponent's half using a reverse stick stroke. The attacking team can only score a goal if all the team's players have moved into the opponent's half. Goals count only if they are shot from within a specified shooting zone. Goals scored using the reverse stick stroke count as double points. The player (x) cannot return to his own half in order to bring the majority back in favour of the attackers.

3/1

2. Tactics

a) Attack

Use the advantage of a reverse stick stroke; you do not need to bring the ball onto the forehand – this takes time.

b) Defence

Also use the reverse stick stroke in defence; in many situations you will be faster on the ball than the attacker.

3/2

3. Techniques

Hitting a static ball – reverse stick

1. Simply hit the ball into an open area.
2. Hit the ball with a reverse stick stroke through a gap and follow the ball up.
3. With the reverse stick strike the ball clockwise round a triangle.

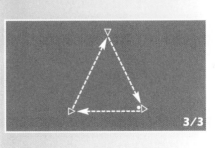

3/3

4. Ball in the Square

The teams stand about 20 m in front of a square as illustrated. Each player has to strike the ball so that it ends up inside the square. *Which team has managed to get the most balls inside the square?*

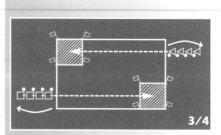

5. Shooting at Goal

Two teams stand opposite each other on a baseline. One after the other the players hit the ball through the goal and over the opponent's game line, which is about 5 m away from the baseline. *Which team manages to get all of its balls over the opposing game line first?*

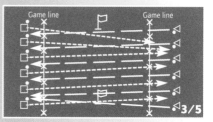

6. Four Goal Game

The players stand round in a circle. Inside the circle a goalkeeper defends a four goal area set-up (see illustration), which he may not enter. The players in the circle try to shoot a goal using the reverse stick stroke. After a specified time the goalkeeper is changed over. *Which goalkeeper saves the most goals?*

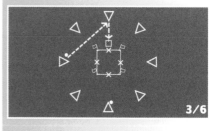

4. Description of the movements

Hitting a static ball – reverse stick

1. The right shoulder points in the direction of the hit.
2. The feet are positioned in a broad straddled position at right angles to the direction of the hit.
3. The left hand firmly grasps the top of the stick with the back of the hand pointing in the direction of the ground.
4. The right hand grasps the stick directly under the left hand with the back of it pointing in the direction of the hit.
5. The stick is angled at about 25° to the ground.
6. The ball lies between and at a distance of approximately 3/4 of the length of the stick in front of the feet.
7. The knees are bent slightly; body centre of balance held low.
8. The upper arms are pushed out slightly from the body.
9. The lower arms are stretched out
10. The stick is pulled back no higher than hip height.
11. When pulled back the toe of the stick end points downwards and the flat side of the stick is held vertically to the ground.
12. The wrists and the left lower arm are angled more than the right arm
13. Change of the centre of balance onto the rear (left) leg.
14. As the ball is hit the centre of balance moves from the rear leg onto the forward leg.
15. The flat side of the stick head strikes the ball at the bottom of the swing.
16. The stick is followed through straight behind the ball.
17. Actively brake the stick in the flat follow through movement; maximum height at hip level.
18. At the end of the swing the toe of the stick end points downwards; the flat side of the stick is vertical to the ground.

5. Incorrect movements

Hitting a static ball – reverse stick

1. Wrong reverse stick grip.
2. The toe of the stick end points up to 'heaven' when being pulled back.
3. You miss the ball, stick passes over it.
4. You hit the ground.
5. You hit (slice) the top of the ball.
6. The stick is lifted above hip height when pulling back.
7. The stick is lifted above hip height in the follow through phase.
8. The stick is lifted above shoulder height (dangerous play – see earlier).
9. The ball doesn't run in the desired direction.
10. Wrong centre of balance.

6. Corrective measures

Hitting a static ball – reverse stick

1. Grasp the stick with the left hand in the basic hold position; the back of the hand should point upwards; place the right hand directly next to it.
2. Turn the toe of the stick end so that it points to the ground.
3. Get nearer to the ball.
4. Move further away from the ball.
5. Don't bend the arms so much; they should be stretched out as you hit the ball.
6. Don't lift the stick above hip height when pulling back
7. Consciously control the stick at hip height.
8. Don't swing the stick above shoulder height (foul play).
9. Bring the stick straight down and not in an arched movement; run the stick along a straight line.

10. Don't remain standing with the centre of balance on the rear leg.

7. The rules

1. When enforced stoppages occur, the time will be taken and added onto the half time of play when the stoppage occurred. (FP/MH/I).
2. Causes of enforced stoppages are:
   - Penalty flick/stroke
   - Injury
   - Player wasting time
   - Unforeseen circumstances

8. The laws

Length of game

Outdoor hockey – Two periods of 35 mins each.

For Junior age groups the duration will normally be shorter.

Indoor hockey is normally played with each half lasting between 10-15 mins according to age group.

2.2.5 Exercising in Zones with Two Goal Mouths

1. The game

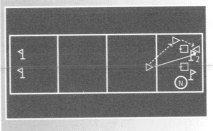

The game is played with a 2:3 attack minority achieved by using neutral players. The playing area is sectioned off into several zones. The attacking team can only reach the next zone by passing the ball, otherwise the ball is turned over to the opposing team. A goal can only be scored once it reaches the last zone. When a goal is scored the ball is turned over to the defending team. This team begins the game in the zone where its own goal is. The neutral player (marked "N") always belongs to the defending team.

2. Tactics

a) Attack

Seek out the best placed player in your team. Play the ball early; it is always faster than you can run! Once you have played the ball: follow up. Play around the defence by using well executed passes. Pass the ball onto and in front of your player otherwise he has to stop to gather it.

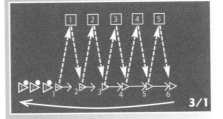

3/1

b) Defence

Be careful! Note that in this game goals can be scored from behind the goal mouth. Try to block the opponent's pass options to the next zone in order to prevent him reaching your goal zone. The opponent will be trying to get round you with his pass – position yourself to prevent this.

3. Techniques

Passing on the move

1. Practice passing to a static player; forehand and reverse stick. Change over groups.

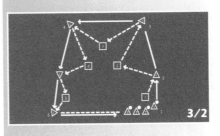

3/2

2. Play around a pyramid so that long and short passes are practiced. Change over groups.
3. Passing the ball in a lane (forehand and reverse stick) by crossing over the lane for the reverse stick shot and occasionally not crossing over.

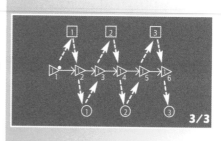

4. Passing in an external circle
With two circles of players inside each other, the outer one rotates while the inside one stands still. Each player in the outer circle plays a ball to one in the inner circle. If a ball goes wild then it is brought back into play where it left the circle. After two or three goes, the players changeover. *Which group manages to achieve 1,2,3...goes first?*

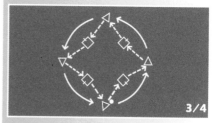

5. Relay race
The players stand in two rows and pass the ball to each other using the forehand or reverse stick strokes. The pairs run to the other end passing as they go. The next pair cannot start until the first pair have crossed a marked-out line at the other end. *Which group wins the relay race?*

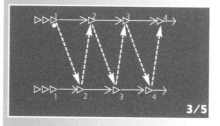

6. Passing by numbers
At least two groups are formed. The players run around in a laid out area. Each player has a number. The players pass the ball to each other in an order which has been worked out beforehand. *Which group has got through all it's numbers first?*

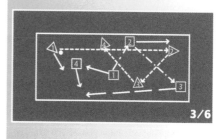

4. Description of the movements

a) Receiving the ball on the move/
forehand

1. Hold the stick as per the forehand grip.
2. When running hold the stick in front of the body.
3. The flat side of the stick points to the left; the toe of the stick head points upwards.
4. When receiving the ball the stick is held at about 45° to the ground.
5. The stick end is held slightly angled to the left in the direction of the approaching ball; hold the position of the stick to protect the ball.
6. Receive the ball in front of the centre of your body; right foot forward.
7. Cushion the ball as it arrives in order to avoid it bouncing off the stick.
8. Gain immediate control of the ball after contact to permit the next action to flow on.
9. The upper body is turned slightly to the left.
10. Keep your eye on the approaching ball.

b) Receiving the ball on the move/
reverse stick

1. Hold the stick as per the reverse stick grip.
2. When running hold the stick in front of the body.
3. Turn the stick into the reverse stick position; the toe of the stick head points downwards towards the ground.
4. When receiving the ball, the stick is held at about 45° to the ground.
5. The flat side of the stick points to the right.
6. The stick end is held slightly angled to the right in the direction of the approaching ball.

Basic grip

Turn grip

Hitting grip

Basic grip viewed from the front

75

7. Receive the ball in front of the centre of your body; left foot forward.
8. Cushion the ball as it arrives in order to avoid it bouncing off the stick.
9. Gain immediate control of the ball after contact to permit the next action to flow on.
10. The upper body is turned slightly to the right.
11. Keep your eye on the approaching ball.

5. Incorrect movements

Receiving the ball on the move – forehand/reverse stick

1. The pass is taken too close to the player (FH/RS)
2. The ball has to be collected too far out to the left of the body (FH)/ to the right of the body (RS) – thus making ball control difficult.
3. The ball jumps over the end of the stick (FH/RS).
4. The ball bounces off the stick head (FH/RS).
5. Turn grip not correct (RS).
6. The stick is not gripped properly for the reverse stick hold (RS).
7. Poor anticipation of the direction of the ball (FH/RS).

6. Corrective measures

Receiving the ball on the move – forehand/reverse stick

1. Reduce your running speed (FH/RS).
2. Collect the ball more on the right foot (FH) or left foot (RS) as appropiate.
3. Take up a more pronounced portective angle of the stick over the ball, to the left (FH) or to the right (RS) as appropiate.
4. Hold the stick more loosely with the right hand (FH/RS).

5. Turn the back of the left hand further upwards (RS).
6. Turn the stick head so that it points towards the ground (RS).
7. Make a conscious effort to follow the ball with your eyes – practice doing this (FH/RS).

7. The rules

1. A goal is scored when the ball completely passes over the goal line underneath the cross-bar between the goal posts. Prerequisite is that you must have played the ball from inside the 'D' (shooting circle) or the ball has been deflected off your stick while you are in this area. This is irrespective of whether the ball has been touched by one or more defenders. (FP/MH/I).
2. If the ball passes over the goal line after you have struck it or passed it from a position outside the shooting circle, then the goal is not counted – even if a defender or the goalkeeper inside the shooting circle has made contact with the ball. If a defender has touched the ball the umpire will award a corner for the attacker (if deliberate it will be a short corner/ if inadvertently a long corner), or a 16 yard push out for the defenders if no defender has touched it (FP). For mini hockey and indoor he awards a restart.

8. The laws

The goal

Outdoor hockey goal/Mini hockey goal
The size of the goal for indoor hockey is the same as that for handball. For mini hockey the handball goal mouth can be used in regional games.

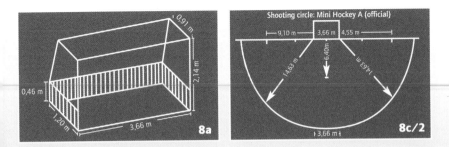

8a

Shooting circle: Mini Hockey A (official)

9,10 m — 3,66 m — 4,55 m

14.63 m — 6,40 m — 14.63 m

3,66 m

8c/2

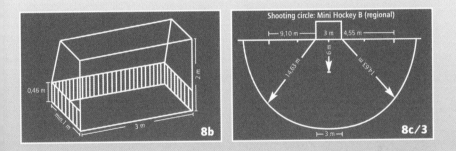

8b

Shooting circle: Mini Hockey B (regional)

9,10 m — 3 m — 4,55 m

14.63 m — 6 m — 14.63 m

3 m

8c/3

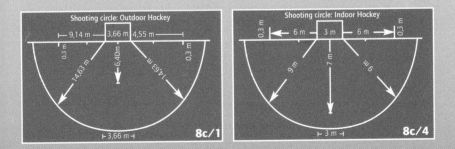

Shooting circle: Outdoor Hockey

9,14 m — 3,66 m — 4,55 m

0,3 m — 14.63 m — 6,40 m — 14.63 m — 0,3 m

3,66 m

8c/1

Shooting circle: Indoor Hockey

0,3 — 6 m — 3 m — 6 m — 0,3 m

9 m — 7 m — 9 m

3 m

8c/4

2.2.6 Exercising with Five Goal Mouths

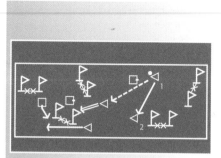

1. The game

The teams are of equal size. Each team can aim at any of the goals, from both sides. To score a second goal a different goal must be aimed at, except when, in the meanwhile, a defender has played the ball. The game is played continuously without breaks. If the ball goes out it is returned into play with a roll-in.

2. Tactics

a) Attack

Don't stay rooted to one spot. Make space for yourself by getting away from the defender. Keep moving about to the unmarked areas. In this way you create new problems for the defence. Give yourself room to receive passes; this gives your team better options for scoring a goal. The more players there are moving about without the ball, the more there are options to pass to them. The player who is standing best placed nearest the goal is the one to receive the ball to shoot at goal.

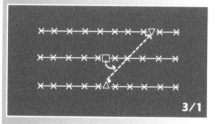

b) Defence

You must be prepared to adjust to a constantly changing defensive situation. Don't let an attacker run in behind your back otherwise you will lose sight of him. An attacker positioned behind a defender can easily exploit every defensive mistake and shoot at goal. Even after a goal has been scored against you, double your efforts to regain control of the ball – your opponents won't freely hand it over!

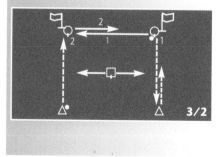

3. Techniques

Seeking unmarked positions

1. Unmarked positions on three lines (2:1).
2. Unmarked positions between 2 marker flags (3:1).
3. Unmarked (3:1).

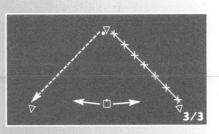

4. Game with two goal mouths

One defender guards two goal mouths, which are positioned at right angles to each other. Three unmarked players constantly move around shooting the ball at the goal from both sides. After a specific time the defender is changed over. *Which combination of the group shoots the most goals?*

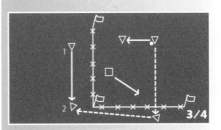

5. Game with a cordoned off area

Three attackers play against one defender with two goal mouths positioned with the openings facing outwards. The attackers may only move round in the framework of the playing area, while the defender can use the inner cordoned off area in order to shorten the distance as he defends. Each of the attackers changes places with the defender once. *Which formation scores the most goals?*

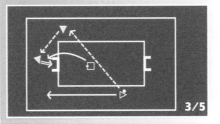

6. Playing the Kingpin

Three players try to shoot a goal at any of three open goals. A fourth player defends the goals. One of the attackers is the "Kingpin" – when he scores, it counts as a double goal. Thus the Kingpin tries to seek unmarked positions as often as possible so that he is free to receive a pass and can shoot at goal. Each player takes on the role of Kingpin once and defender also once. *Which group scores the most goals?*

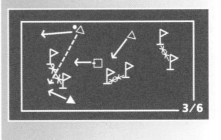

79

4. Description of the movements

Unmarked play

1. The player with the ball and the player receiving the ball should attempt to remain unmarked in a triangular area.
2. The angle between the player who will receive the ball and the player with the ball should be greater than 90° (obtuse-angled triangle).
3. A defensive player will be able to prevent a pass if the angle is less than 90° (acute-angled triangle).

5. Incorrect movements

Unmarked play

1. You cannot pass to the player.
2. The opponent can intercept the pass.
3. The opponent can cut out the pass.

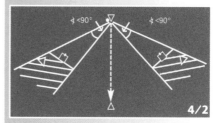

6. Corrective measures

Unmarked play

1. You are standing on the same spot too long. Move around more in free areas.
2. You are badly positioned relative to the passer. Run towards the passer so that an obtuse-angle is created.
3. You have waited too long before passing the ball; the optimum moment to pass the ball has been lost. In such situations pass earlier.

7. The rules

1. When the ball completely crosses the sideline it is out of play and it must be brought into play again at the point (on the sideline) where it went out by being hit or pushed back into play. (FP/MH).
2. In indoor hockey the ball must be placed up to 1 m away from where it jumped over the sideboards (see p. 112), and pushed in from there. (I).
3. If the ball was hit or pushed over the home goal line by an opponent, then the ball is brought back into play by using a push from a spot opposite where the ball went out (no further than 16 yards (14.63 m) away from the goal-line). No opponent may approach nearer than 5 m. (FP/MH).
4. In indoor hockey the game is restarted by using a push shot from any point inside the shooting circle. At that moment opponents may not be inside the shooting circle. (I).

9. The laws

Age groups will depend on the local national rulings. In Germany for example from the year 2000 youths are divided into the following age groups:

Boys/Girls D	up to 8 years old
Boys/Girls C	9-10 years old
Boys/Girls B	11-12 years old
Boys/Girls A	13-14 years old
Males/Females Youth B	15-16 years old
Males/Females Youth A	17-18 years old
Juniors (Male/Female)	19-21 years old

2.3 Game Situation 3 Working out Goal Scoring Situations - Preventing Goals

2.3.1 Parallel Games with Four Goals

1. The game

The game is played with a 3:2 attack majority. Each team tries to build up goal opportunities on two goals while defending two goals. Goals can only be scored from within the shooting zone. Players may not be specifically assigned to defending a particular goal. The ball must be dribbled across the centre line. If it is hit across the centre line the ball is passed over to the other team who continue the game from their half. One attacker (marked 'x') always remains in the opponent's half to maintain a majority.

2. Tactics

a) Attack

You can dribble the ball using the forehand grip. Use the width of the pitch. Make use of the wings as there are better opportunities to be able to build a score up from here.

b) Defence

Two goals have to be defended while you are in a minority and as a result the defence may lose cohesion. Overcome this disadvantage by shielding the goal areas.

3. Techniques

Forehand dribbling going round to the left

1. Dribble forehand with the ball in a left handed curve around skittles/marker flags etc.

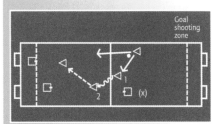

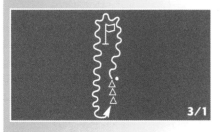

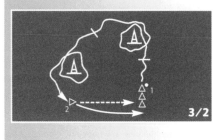

2. Dribble forehand with variations of stopping, turning in a left-handed curve and passing.

3. Dribble forehand with variations of turning in a left-handed curve, stopping, pulling back and shooting at goal.

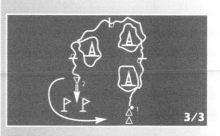

4. Starting and stopping

The players stand back to back on a centre line. On a command from the exercise leader the players run in pairs round an object. *Who returns to his starting position first? Which group managed to complete the exercise first?*

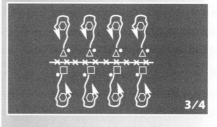

5. The Astronaut Game

The players move around on 'Earth' (a circle). At a command they leave Earth and journey to their 'Planet' (round a flag marker) and return to Earth. *Who lands safe and sound back on Earth first?*

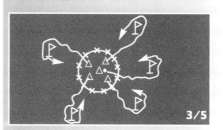

6. Six-day Race

Two players form a team. Each team has to run a previously agreed number of laps. Players change over in a laid-down changeover area. The frequency of changeover is decided individually by each team (i.e., after 1, 2 or 3 laps). (Count out loud as each lap is completed). *Which team completes the full number of laps first?*

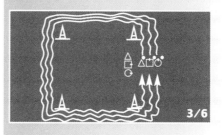

4. Description of the move-
ments
a) Dribbling the ball forehand
1. The player's stance points in the direction of movement.
2. The stick is held slanting in the forehand grip in front of the body; the flat side of the stick is pointing forwards in the running direction.
3. The stick is angled at 45° to the ground.
4. The left hand grips the stick in the basic position and the right hand is placed 2-2½ hand's width below, just like in the forehand push pass.
5. The left lower arm forms a straight line with the stick; both wrists grip loosely.
6. The ball is positioned about 1-1½ feet lengths away from the right foot, directly in front of the stick.
7. Knock the ball forward by tapping or touching it lightly in the direction of movement (indoors move the ball by pushing the stick head along the floor).
8. The right shoulder must be lower than the left one.
9. Don't look at the ball.

b) Stopping the ball
1. Stop running and stand with the left foot forward.
2. Change the centre of balance on to the rear right leg in order to increase the ability of the left leg to provide a fulcrum action.
3. The left hand changes to a turn grip; form an eyelet with the right hand.
4. Turn the stick head into the reverse stick position; in doing so bring the stick head over the ball and place it in front of the ball.
5. Stop the ball about level with the left foot and at the side of the body.

c) Pulling back the ball

1. Pull the ball back from the forward foot to the rear foot while the legs are positioned apart.
2. Bring the stick into the reverse stick position in front of the ball.
3. The right hand pulls the stick backwards.
4. Turn the stick head into the forehand position.
5. Place the stick head behind the ball and stop the ball.
6. Change the centre of balance from the forward leg on to the rear leg in order to increase the fulcrum action.
7. Run forward, taking up the ball in the forehand position.

d) Moving in a left-handed curve

1. Bring the ball in front of the body from the sideways forehand position.
2. The left elbow is kept well into the body; the right arm is stretched out.
3. The flat side of the stick points to the left and forwards.
4. Move the ball to the left into a curve; the stick head stays in contact with the ball.
5. The left hand presses down on the top of the stick; the right hand traces a curving motion (change of direction).
6. The player keeps up with the ball with small steps.
7. At the end of the curve, play the ball on with the stick held in a forehand position.

5. Incorrect movements
Dribble forehand / stopping / pulling back / left-handed curve

1. The right hand holds the top of the stick.
2. The stick is angled greater than 45° to the ground.

3. The ball is dribbled too close to the body and, as a result the running rhythm is broken and the player steps on the ball.
4. The player's upper body is bent too much; lack of overview of play.
5. The left hand is not in the turn grip.
6. The right hand twists at the same time.
7. The stick is held too vertically.
8. The ball rolls on because the stick head was not brought far enough over it.
9. Not enough pressure is exercised by the left hand so that the ball does not move in a curving motion.
10. Prior to the curving movement the speed of the ball was too high; the player cannot keep up with the ball.
11. The centre of balance was not placed onto the rear leg sufficiently.

6. Corrective measures

Dribble forehand / stopping / pulling back / left-handed curve

1. Make sure you grip the stick top with the left hand and with the right hand grasp farther down.
2. Push the top of the stick further towards the ground; form a 45° angle with it.
3. Push the ball further away sideways to the body; make sure there is at least a gap of one length of your foot.
4. Lift the upper part of your body more upright so that you have a better overview of your position.
5. Turn the back of the hand more upwards.
6. Make an eyelet with the right hand.
7. Push the top of the stick further towards the ground; move the lower left arm so that it forms a prolongation of the stick.

8. Put the stick head on the ground in front of the ball.
9. Push the top of the stick further away from the body; adopt a better angled stick position; move the ball in a curving movement with the right hand and pull the left one back.
10. Reduce the speed of the ball, if necessary by using the stopping movement.
11. Place the centre of balance over the rear leg.

7. The rules

1. Doing a left-handed curve movement should not cause any difficulty in making sure you use the flat side of the stick. (FP/MH/I).
2. When stopping the ball you may only use the flat side of the stick otherwise you will commit a stick fault. (FP/MH/I).
3. When you pull back the ball, you may only, similarly, use the flat side of the stick – if not it will be a stick fault. (FP/MH/I).

8. The laws

The Umpire

A good umpire has the following qualities

↓	↓	↓
Fitness	Fairness	Knowledge of the rules
Concentration	Impartiality	Interpreting the rules
Reaction	Sportsmanlike	Good overview
Mobility	Courage	Thinking ahead
Positional play	Self-confidence	Intuitive understanding

2.3.2 A Game with Side-line Goal Mouths

1. The game

The game is played as an attacking game with an attack majority of 3:2. Each team plays against two goal mouths, one on the base-line and one on the side-line and has to defend two similar goals in it's own half. None of the goal mouths may be defended by a specifically assigned goalkeeper. The ball must be dribbled across the diagonal line otherwise the ball is passed over to the opposing team. The attacker (x) stays in the attacking triangular zone to maintain the majority.

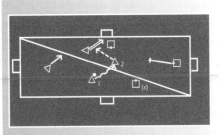

2. Tactics

a) Attack

Attack the goal on the side-line. If you target this goal the defence will lose it's coherence.

b) Defence

The opponent can also play against the goal on the side-line; as a result you will have to deploy your defence differently – guard both goals. You must make sure that you cover the gaps. You are playing in a large area with a minority; use long shots and passes. Push the opponent back to where his goals are situated.

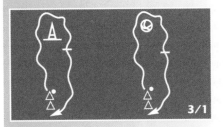

3/1

3/2

3. Techniques

Forehand dribble in a right-handed curve

1. Dribble on the forehand going in a right-handed curve running round a marker flag/skittle/ball etc., and stop.

2. Dribble on the forehand in a right-handed curve, changing to reverse stick dribbling, stopping and passing.

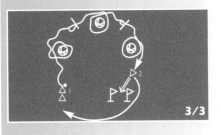

3/3

87

3. Dribble on the forehand in a right-handed curve, changing to reverse stick dribbling, stopping and shooting at a goal.

4. The Concertina Game
The players stand behind a start line and all go together on the exercise leader's command. They dribble, to the first, second, third flag marker – dependent on the command given – and run round the marker in a right-handed curve. Variation: Each time the players run to the first marker and back and then to the second etc. *Who completes the course first?*

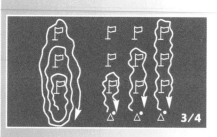

5. The number race
The players stand lined-up in a star formation. Players on each side of the star receive a number. When the exercise leader gives the command all the players with that number run forward clockwise to the next star flank. *Who reaches his starting point again first? Which group completes the course first?*

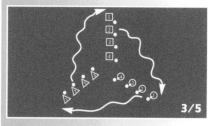

6. The chasing game
The players form up on the opposite sides of a square. The first player starts off, clockwise, and runs round the square and passes the ball to the next player in his team, and so on. *Which group can overtake the other?*

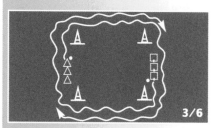

4. Description of the movements
a) Right-handed curve, running over the ball and forehand dribbling
1. Dribble the ball on the forehand.
2. Run past the ball so that it is at the back of your stance.

3. Bring the left elbow forward.
4. Pull the right shoulder back and lower it.
5. Pull the stick back and collect the ball on a level with the ankle.
6. Turn the stick head outwards (to the right).
7. Push the ball to the right into a curve; the stick head remains in contact with the ball.
8. The left hand pushes down on the top of the stick; adopt a smaller stick angle position to protect the ball.
9. Take the ball on with the stick head into a curving movement.
10. After completing the curve, use small steps to get back into dribbling on the forehand.

b) Right-handed curve using reverse stick dribbling

1. Dribble the ball on the forehand.
2. Bring the ball round in front of the body from the forehand dribble.
3. Hold the left hand in the turn position.
4. Form an eyelet with the right hand.
5. Turn the stick into the reverse stick hold.
6. Hold the right elbow close into the body.
7. Stretch the left arm out and press down on top of the stick.
8. Using the reverse stick grip pull the ball into a curve with the right hand (change of direction); the stick head remains in contact with the ball.
9. The flat side of the stick points forwards and to the right.
10. Using short steps the player stays behind the ball.
11. After completing the curve get back into dribbling on the forehand.

89

5. Incorrect movements

Right-handed curve

1. The player does not run round the ball.
2. The player cannot run over the ball because the speed of the ball is too high.
3. When collecting the ball the stick is slanted backwards and the ball jumps over the stick head.
4. In a right-handed curve the ball is played with the rounded side of the stick.
5. The stick is too upright; the ball is too close to the body.
6. The stick head is not kept on the ground; the ball cannot be brought under control any more.
7. The curving motion cannot be carried out because the top end of the stick is too close to the body.

6. Corrective measures

Right-handed curve

1. Take faster and shorter steps.
2. Slow down the speed of the ball; place the stick in front of the ball for a second.
3. With the left hand push the top end of the stick slightly forward.
4. Turn the stick into the reverse stick hold; the tip of the stick head points towards the ground.
5. Press the top of the stick more towards the ground; form an angle of 45°; the left lower arm and the stick should be in a straight line.
6. Press the stick head onto the ground deliberately.
7. Increase your distance to the ball.

7. The rules

1. You must use the flat side of the stick even in a right-handed curve. (FP/MH/I). Watch out – there is a danger that it is too easy to use the wrong (rounded) side of the stick.
2. If you inadvertently touch the ball with the backside of the stick, without creating an advantage for yourself, the umpire will not necessarily blow for the fault. But don't count on it! On no occasion may you play the ball with the rounded side of the stick (FP/MH/I).

8. The laws

Control of the game by two umpires and two time-keepers

Two umpires control the game. Each umpire is responsible for play in his half and along his sideline. Some of the further points in the game are the corner, penalty corner, penalty stroke and a goal decision. The umpires are responsible for the length of playing time and time outs. The time-keepers keep the time and indicate the end of play for each half.

2.3.3 Four-corner Goal Games

1. The game

The game is played with 2:3 attack minority. Each team has to attack one of the goals in a corner or defend it accordingly. None of the goal mouths is specifically defended by an assigned player. Goals can only be scored from within the shooting zone. The centre line must be crossed by a dribbling movement, otherwise the ball is passed over to the opponents and the game continues from their half. One of the defenders (x) stays in his own half in order to maintain the minority.

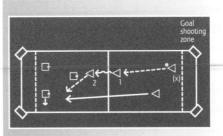

2. Tactics

a) Attack

Keep the ball under control. When dribbling you can protect the ball with your stick. Only dribble whenever you cannot pass to your partner. **N.B.** Pass rather than dribble! Dribbling gives you only a temporary advantage in certain situations. Get rid of the ball as fast as you can. Don't be tempted to do unnecessary dribbling – the opponents can use the time to quickly reform.

b) Defence

Get back into defence quickly if you lose the ball. Unnecessary dribbling by your opponents will allow you to reform better in your own defensive area. Don't be the last man on your side to dribble; each time you lose the ball can mean a chance for the opponent to score.

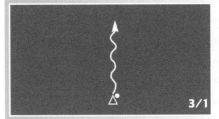

3/1

3. Techniques

Introduction to dribbling

1. Practice dribbling standing still, walking and at the trot.

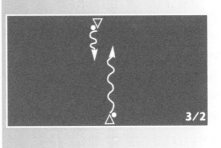

3/2

2. Dribble together with your partner alternately while running to a new position where he changes over with you.
3. Dribble the ball in a straight line with your partner or within your group.

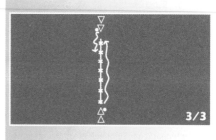

3/3

4. *Moving the ball to a point and collecting it again*

The players line up behind each other. The first one in the line-up dribbles the ball to a point and runs back to the starting point without the ball. The second player runs to the ball and dribbles it back to the start point. Carry this on until all the players have had a go. *Which group completes 1,2,3... rounds the fastest?*

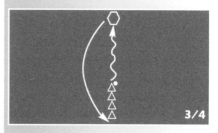

3/4

5. *Passing the "Parcel" (the ball)*

The players stand in a lane offset from each other. The first player dribbles the ball to the next player opposite and takes his place. The second player takes on the ball and dribbles it on to the next player and so on until all the players have gone through. If a player loses the "parcel" (the ball) the game is continued from where he lost it. *Which group passes the parcel the fastest?*

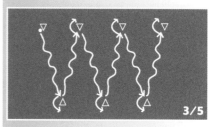

3/5

6. *Beat the tackler*

The players stand in two rows with a gap between each row. On a command the players in the first row try to dribble the ball to a marker while the players in the second row try to tackle them. If the first row player, who is dribbling, reaches the marker, he returns to his start position. If he is tackled then the players change places. *Who manages to dribble the ball to the marker?*

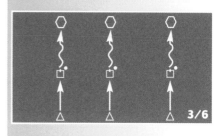

3/6

4. Description of the movements

Dribbling the ball in front of the body

1. The player runs forward.
2. The left hand holds the stick in the turn grip.
3. The right hand holds the stick as for the forehand push pass at a point 1-2 hand-widths lower down on the grip rubber.
4. The right hand holds the stick loosely with an eyelet ready to turn the stick onto the reverse stick position.
5. The stick forms a 45° angle to the ground.
6. The ball lies between and in front of the feet about 1 1/2 lengths of the foot away.
7. The flat side of the stick is on the right of the ball and next to it.
8. Play the ball forwards with the forehand (to begin with slightly diagonally and forward).
9. Turn the stick into the reverse stick position.
10. The flat side of the stick is close to the left side of the ball after the stick head has been brought over the ball.
11. Play the ball forwards with the reverse stick (to begin with slightly diagonally and forward).
12. Turn the stick into the forehand stick position – when doing so the stick head comes over the ball onto the right side of the ball.
13. Keep repeating the movements in steps 7-12 above.
14. Each time you make contact with the ball move it forward.
15. Keep the ball going in a straight line.
16. Play the ball so far in front of the body that you have to keep your arms stretched out.
17. When the speed of the ball increases dribble the ball further away from the body.

18. As you make contact with the ball on the forehand your **right** foot is forward.
19. As you make contact with the ball on the reverse stick your **left** foot is forward.
20. Keep your eyes up in order to widen your field of vision.

5. Incorrect movements
Dribbling the ball

1. The ball is played too diagonally and it runs along the ground like a snake.
2. The left hand is not positioned in the turn grip.
3. The left wrist is angled to the left lower arm; a rapid turn cannot be carried out.
4. The right hand turns at the same time; the upper body is twisted too much.
5. The reverse stick slows the ball down.
6. The player steps on the ball; wrong rhythm.
7. The ball does not receive sufficient impetus; the stick strikes the upper edge of the ball.
8. The eyes are not lifted up from the ball.

6. Corrective measures
Dribbling the ball

1. Lead the ball in a straight line.
2. The back of the hand must be pointing upwards.
3. Loosely stretch out the left hand.
4. Form an eyelet with the right hand; your upper body will no longer twist at the same time.
5. Turn the stick completely into the reverse stick hold and place the stick head closer to the ball.

6. Say the rhythm out loud (FH/RS) and slowly come from a standing position into a walk and then break into a run.
7. Deliberately place the stick head on the ground (ground contact).
8. Dribble the ball in a narrow area, and take notice of the things around you.

7. The rules

1. Even when you are dribbling you must use the flat side of the stick. (FP/MH/I).
2. When dribbling there is always a danger that you play the ball with the rounded side of the stick and this counts as a stick fault. Hockey is not like Ice-hockey. (FP/MH/I).

8. The laws
When should the umpire blow his whistle?
The umpire stops the game:

- At the beginning and at the end of each half of play.
- When there is an infringement.
- To allow a penalty flick or stroke to be taken or to end it.
- To indicate when a goal has been scored.
- To award a penalty corner.
- To stop play for any other reason e.g., for an accident.
- To indicate that the ball has crossed out of play when this is not obvious.

94

2.3.4 Games with Four Goals Placed Freely in the Area

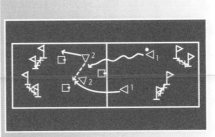

1. The game

Team sizes are equal. Each team plays against two open goals and have to defend two others themselves. The ball must be dribbled over the centre line, otherwise the ball is passed over to the other team in their half. A goal can be scored from either side of the goal mouth. A second goal, however, must be scored in another goal mouth unless the opponents have touched the ball beforehand.

2. Tactics

a) Attack

If you turn the stick quickly, you can play on the ball using the dribble without the opponent intervening. You can control the ball easier when you keep your eyes up and not down on the ball (peripheral vision). You can take exact note of the opponent's defensive actions. If there is no one free to pass to you can keep the ball moving on your own side by dribbling.

3/1

b) Defence

Don't dribble in your own shooting zone. A simple mistake will lead to giving the opponent extra chances to score a goal.

3. Techniques

Perfecting the dribble

1. Simultaneous dribbling of the ball along a straight line/a marked out route/ round a circle made out by your partner.
2. Slalom dribbling through rows of skittles /balls/marker flags with changeover of groups.

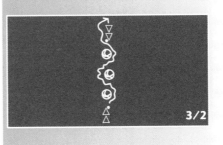

3/2

3. Dribbling while changing sides to two or four sides.

4. "Change trees"

The game is arranged so that there is one home base (a marker flag) less than the number of players. The player who has no marker to occupy calls out "Change trees!". At this command the other players try to reach, dribbling a ball, another marker. The player who misses out finding a marker can call out for another change to be made and so on. *Who is the quickest to find his marker?*

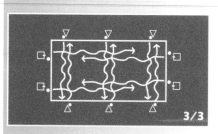

5. Moving house

Each player occupies a "house" which he changes over with a partner. The "houses" are areas on the outside of a circle formed around a middle point. On the exercise leader's command the players dribble the ball across the circle. *Which partners have 'moved house' the fastest without losing the ball?*

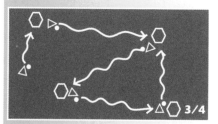

6. Day and Night

Two teams – 'Day' and 'Night' – stand in lanes opposite each other. Each player has a ball. The exercise leader calls out either "Day!" or "Night!". The team called out has to chase (without a ball) the retreating team (who are dribbling) and tackle the ball off them before they reach a marked-off line. The retreating team has to go back straight and cannot dodge about. *Who manages to dribble their ball over the line?*

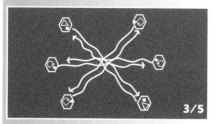

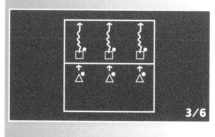

96

a) Indoor hockey stick with thinner flattened stick head

b) Outdoor hockey stick with thickened stick head

c) Outdoor hockey ball with a seam

d) Indoor hockey ball without a seam

4. The rules

1. Note that contact with the opponent's stick or body is forbidden (FP/MH/I).

2. N.B. Hockey is not a contact sport.

3. You are not allowed to strike the opponent's stick, hook at it, hold it down or thrust at him with your own stick (FP/MH/I).

4. Also, you may not throw your stick at the ball (FP/MH/I).

Goalkeeper Equipment

Helmet

Face Mask

Chest Protector

Abdominal Protector

Gloves

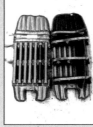

Leg Pads

Kickers

5. The laws

Signs given by the umpire

1. Goal
2. Penalty flick/stroke
3. Penalty corner
4. Corner (only outdoor hockey)
5. Free hit/Push in
6. Free hit closer than 5 m to the defender's shooting circle (only outdoor hockey)
7. Hit off
8. Push in/Hit in
9. Break in play
10. Restart/Bully (off)
11. Advantage
12. Foot fault
13. Obstruction
14. Dangerous play, rough play and/or bad (unfair) behaviour
15. Start play
16. Lifted Ball
17. Advancement of the free hit
18. Ball at penalty corner

98

2.4 Game Situation 4 Building up the Game - Closing down the Game

2.4.1 Game with Free Channels

1. The game

The game is played with an attacking advantage of 3:2. The pitch is divided into three channels, of which two are narrow ones – free channels. The attacking team may not be challenged in the free channels. This serves to allow them to switch their play to these outside channels more easily. Goals may only be scored from within the shooting zones. One defender (x) stays in his own half to ensure the majority. There is no goalkeeper assigned.

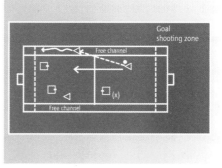

2. Tactics

a) Attack

If you want to dribble round an opponent you must be able to kick off better than he does. The higher your speed as you play round him, the more your distance from the opponent has to be; you can trick your opponent with a change of tempo and direction. Watch out for the other opponents prior to going round the opponent; they could get to the ball quicker than you can. Be careful not to cause an obstruction when going round.

b) Defence

To go round you, the opponent must lead up to increasing his speed early on; this way you can predict his intention. The attacker will try to distract you – mark him carefully. Every time the ball is lost – even in your opponent's half – the defence begins. Disrupting his play will unnerve him; start doing this as early as possible.

3. Techniques

Running round by pushing past

1. Using a push pass run round an object (passive opponent – marker flag/small box with a hockey stick stuck in it/chair/ball etc.) on the forehand or the reverse stick.

2. Using a push pass run round an object (passive opponent) keeping it at a distance (indicated by using a hockey stick/ hoop/ skittle to mark the gap), on the forehand or the reverse stick, and passing to a partner followed by running to a new position.

3. Using a push pass run round a semi-active opponent (indicated by him placing a foot on a ball skittle etc) and keeping one pace distance from him or/and waving his stick. After passing him on the forehand or the reverse stick, collecting up the ball and shooting at goal, concluding by returning to the start position.

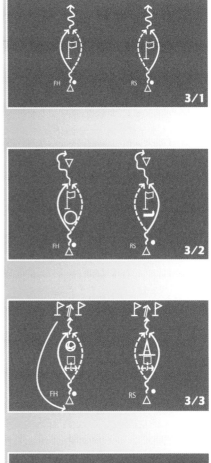

4. American Football

The attackers try to reach the next zone, just like in American Football. The defender is semi-active i.e., he is fixed with his foot resting on a skittle. After a successful push pass the attacker runs on to the next zone. If the defender is successful in warding the attack off he sets himself at the beginning again and is the first to be played against on the next turn. The teams changeover roles after a specific time. *Which team manages to push past the most?*

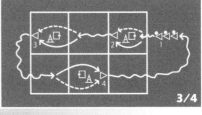

5. The shepherd

One of the players (the shepherd) stands at

one end of the pitch; the other players (the sheep) stand waiting on the other side. When the shepherd calls out they run across the pitch to the other side. The shepherd tries to 'catch' the sheep (take the ball away from them). Any sheep caught join in the game again. After a specific time the shepherd is replaced. *Which sheep manage the most crossings of the pitch?*

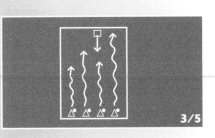

6. The bridge guard

Two bank seats, or two tapes laid on the ground, serve to represent the bridge on which the bridge guard is standing. The players all stand on one side of the bridge. At a signal the players run forward over the bridge, pushing past the guard who tries to take the ball off them. All players remain in the game. Each time the players successfully cross the bridge they get one point. *Which bridge guard has the most points scored against him?*

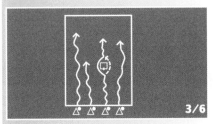

4. Description of the movements

a) Simple push past on the opponent's reverse stick

1. Dribble or move the ball on the forehand.
2. Lift your eyes up away from the ball; keep the opponent in sight.
3. Play the ball past the opponent using the forehand push pass against his reverse stick, or push past with the ball between leg and stick.
4. Speed up and run round past the opponent on his forehand side.
5. Collect the ball again straight away and bring it under control.
6. Play the ball on further.

b) Simple push past on the opponent's forehand

1. Dribble or move the ball on the forehand.
2. Lift your eyes up from the ball; keep the opponent in sight.
3. Collect the ball on the reverse stick.
4. Play the ball past the opponent using the reverse stick push pass against his forehand stick, or push past with the ball between leg and stick.
5. Speed up and run round past the opponent on his reverse stick side.
6. Collect the ball again straight away (ball under control).
7. Play the ball on further.

5. Incorrect movements

Simple push past

1. You are still watching the ball.
2. The ball is pushed forward too soon and the opponent has guessed the intention of the attacker.
3. The push past occurs too late and the opponent can play the ball away.
4. The ball is played too close to the opponent.

6. Corrective measures

Simple push past

1. Watch your opponent!
2. Bring the ball closer to the opponent and then execute the move rapidly.
3. Push the ball at just the right moment so that you can avoid the opponent's sweeping stick or block.
4. Push the ball past the opponent at a greater distance from him.

7. The rules

1. It is forbidden to cause an obstruction between opponent and the ball by using the body or the stick as an obstruction. You may also not obstruct a player from breaking free even if he is not on the ball (e.g., by blocking him). (FP/MH/I).
2. A complete turn of the body on his own axis by a player in possession of the ball doesn't constitute an obstruction, providing the opponent is not prevented from being able to reach the ball.
3. An obstruction is caused when another team member blocks or obstructs an opponent in order to create free room for his own player who has ball possession. (Known also as a "Third Party" obstruction). (FP/MH/I).

8. Note

Actively attempting to protect the ball while between the ball and the opponent is allowed.

103

2.4.2 Wing Play

1. The game

The game is played as a 3:2 majority attacking game. There is a goal mouth in each half (marker flags), which can only be played in one direction in order to score a goal. Goals only count if they are scored in the shooting zone. The player marked "x" stays in the opponent's half in order to maintain a majority.

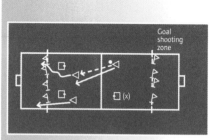

2. Tactics

a) Attack

Using a stick feint (dummy) you can cover the ball effectively. Use the stick dummy as little as possible otherwise the opponent will soon get wise to the trick. Passing the opponent will only bring a temporary advantage; use this quickly and where necessary play the ball on immediately. Only use the dummy when there is no possibility to play the ball on. Don't use the dummy when the opponent is slower; they react to it too late.

b) Defence

Do not be too hasty to attack when playing in defence; you will be an easy target for a dummy movement. Don't stand still if you have been passed round; run after the attacker straight away in order to disrupt his playing actions. Run back towards your own goal in order to cover and mark any gaps created by an attacker who has passed a defender.

3. Techniques

Passing an opponent using the body or stick feint

1. Passing round an object (passive opponent – marker flag etc), feinting with the body/ stick and body on the forehand, or the reverse stick; running on to a new position.

2. Passing round an object (passive opponent), feinting with the body/ stick and body, keeping it at a distance (indicated by using a hoop etc to mark the gap) on the forehand, or the reverse stick, followed by running back to the start position.

3. Passing round a semi-active opponent (indicated by him placing a foot on a skittle or waving his stick) and keeping at a limited distance from him. After passing him on the forehand or the reverse stick, shoot at goal and conclude by returning to the original position.

4. Open sesame!

Each player tries to play through all of the four 'caves' by using a body or stick feint. A successful feint in one cave opens the entrance to the next. If the feint does not work then the attacker changes place with the defender. The player who manages to get through all four caves concludes by shooting at goal and starts all over again. The defender is only partly active. *Who gets as far as being able to shoot at goal?*

5. Changing sides

The players are all lined up on the narrower side of the playing area with a 'catcher' positioned inside the area. The players dribble the ball to the other side of the playing area

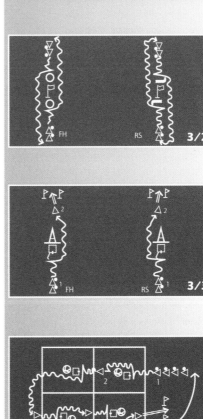

and back. The catcher has to try to prevent them doing this by trying to get the ball off them. Players able to cross over and back without losing the ball get a point. The catcher is changed over after a specific period of time. *Who manages to get the most points?*

6. The Bogey Man
The Bogey Man stands on the one side of the playing area with the players on the other side. The players have to reach the other side still in possession of the ball. The Bogey Man can stop this happening by taking the ball off them, after which they turn into helpers. The player who is last to be caught takes on the role of the Bogey Man. *Who is going to be the Bogey Man?*

4. Description of the movements

a) Passing an opponent at the dribble, feinting with the body on the reverse stick side of the opponent

1. Dribble the ball in front of the body.
2. The stick forms a 45° angle to the ground.
3. Place the stick, holding it in the reverse stick position, to the left side of the ball.
4. The stick head points towards the ground and the flat side of the stick points to the right.
5. Take a short step to the left, bringing your weight temporarily onto the left leg and faking a passing movement on the forehand side of the opponent.
6. Push off hard with the left leg, switching your weight onto the right leg.
7. At the same time pull the ball with the reverse stick diagonally forwards and right (across your path).

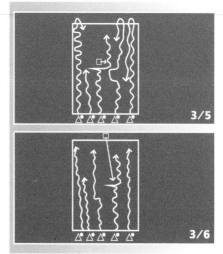

3/5

3/6

8. Collect the ball on the level with the right foot and dribble past the opponent on his reverse stick side and onwards.
9. Run quickly past the opponent on his reverse stick side; make good use of your body feint as you complete it.

b) Passing an opponent at the dribble, feinting with the body and the stick on the reverse stick side of the opponent

1. Dribble the ball in front of the body.
2. The stick forms a 45° angle to the ground.
3. Bring the stick in a circling sweeping motion on the forehand across the ground (floor – in a hall) between the ball – on its left side – and the opponent; then cover the ball with your stick.
4. Place the stick into the reverse stick position; the stick head points towards the ground and the flat side of the stick points to the right.

5. Take a short step to the left bringing your weight temporarily onto the left leg and faking a passing movement on the forehand side of the opponent.
6. Continue as per numbers 6-9 (from 4a) of passing an opponent at the dribble, feinting with the body on the reverse stick side of the opponent.

c) Passing an opponent at the dribble, feinting with the body and the stick on the forehand side of the opponent
1. Dribble the ball in front of the body.
2. The stick forms a 45° angle to the ground.
3. Place the stick, holding it in the forehand position, to the right side of the ball.
4. The stick head points upwards and the flat side of the stick points to the left.
5. Take a short step to the right bringing your weight temporarily onto the right leg and faking a passing movement on the reverse stick side of the opponent.
6. Push off hard with the right leg switching your weight onto the left leg.
7. At the same time push the ball on the forehand stick diagonally forwards and left (across your path).
8. Collect the ball on the level with the left foot and dribble past the opponent on his forehand side and onwards.
9. Run quickly past the opponent on his forehand side; make good use of your body feint as you complete it.

107

5. Incorrect movements

Passing an opponent at the dribble, feinting with the body and the stick on the forehand side

1. The dummy (feint) is made too close i.e., there is no way round any more, or too far away i.e., the opponent recognises the dummy being made.
2. An indistinct side-step; the opponent doesn't react to the dummy; the attacker runs into the defender.
3. While going round on the forehand side the ball has not been properly played with the reverse stick.
4. On the forehand side, the ball has not been properly played forward and to the right.
5. Passing too slowly round the opponent; the defender can react to the movement and run alongside.
6. The stick feint is not played close enough and across the ground; the ball is not covered or not played properly with the reverse stick.

6. Corrective measures

Passing an opponent at the dribble, feinting with the body and the stick on the forehand side

1. Pick your eyes up from the ball early so that you can see your opponent and check your distance to him.
2. Switch your weight more consciously on to your left foot (FH) or right foot (RS); wait for the opponent's reaction.
3. Bring the stick head more into the reverse stick position; the stick head must point towards the ground.
4. Push the top of the stick a little more to the right so that the ball can be collected up diagonally.
5. Accelerate faster and try to dash past the opponent.
6. Make sure the stick head is moved in a circling sweep across the ground; consciously press the head onto the ground.

7. The rules

1. The umpire can decide which side has the advantage. He is not required to punish every infringement. When no disadvantage falls to the opponents, he does not have to blow his whistle. (FP/MH/I).
2. Similarly the umpire can decide not to penalise an infringement if he is convinced that it does not afford an advantage to the side that committed the infringement. (FP/MH/I).

8. The laws

The rule of the advantage

When the ball touches the player's foot or part of his body, it does not necessarily constitute an infringement. Only when there is intentional contact made with the foot or body in order to gain an advantage, is there a case for a penalty. It is not always easy for the umpire to decide whether there has been any intention or not to commit an infringement.

2.4.3 No-go Passing Zone

1. The game

The playing area is divided into two equal halves with a passing zone in the middle. The sidelines are marked with sideboards (functioning like the cushions on a billiard table). The passing zone can only be crossed by passing the ball out of either half or from the sideboards. Players can enter the passing zone but may not touch the ball while in the zone. Play should be built up rapidly. Using the sideboards, a majority can be achieved. Goals may only be scored from within the goal shooting zone. There is no goalkeeper assigned.

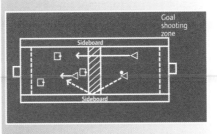

2. Tactics

a) Attack

Use the sideboards when attacking; they are equivalent to having another player on your side. Using the sideboards you can create a majority in the attack. Play onto your own team players by rebounding off the sideboards.

b) Defence

As a defender don't stand too far away from the sideboards. In this way you won't be easily played around. Position yourself so that you can touch the sideboard with your stick in a low down position so that you can effectively block passes.

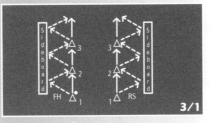

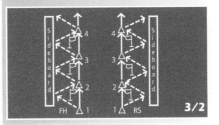

3. Techniques

Passing an opponent using the sideboards

1. Repeatedly play against the sideboards/ laid down bench on the forehand or reverse stick.

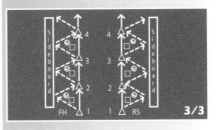

2. Play round consecutively placed, passive opponents (objects – marker flags etc.,) using the sideboard/bench on the forehand or the reverse stick.
3. Play round consecutively placed, partly passive (stick waving) opponents using the sideboard/bench on the opponent's forehand or reverse stick.

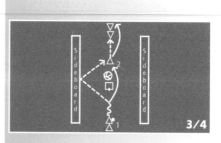

4. Shuttle Relay
By using a shuttle relay the players cross the playing area. The defender in the middle of the area is partially active and has to be played round by using a rebound off the sideboard. If this is not successful then the player lines up from the start again for another attempt. The players have to go through twice – once with a forehand pass and once with a reverse stick pass. *Which team finishes 2-4... goes first?*

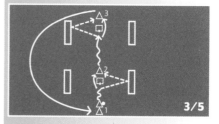

5. Two bridges
The game is played like the Bridge Guard game. The players have to outplay the guard by using a sideboard pass on the forehand or the reverse stick. If a player doesn't reach the other side he has to start from the beginning again. After 1,2,3.... Goes, the guard is changed over. *Who manages to complete the most crossings of the bridges?*

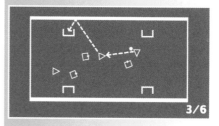

6. The Sideboard Game
Each team tries to score a goal by rebounding off the sideboard. Two goals in each half are used. The goals (using open cardboard boxes) are placed with the open side to the sideboard. *Which team scores the most goals off the sideboards?*

4. Description of the movements

a) Passing an opponent on the forehand using the sideboards, dribbling

1. Dribble the ball in front of the body.
2. The stick forms a 45° angle to the ground.
3. Place the stick, holding it in the forehand position, to the right side of the ball; the flat side of the stick is pointing to the left.
4. Push pass the ball firmly against the sideboard to the left (forehand side of the opponent).
5. By a fast kick off, go round the opponent on his reverse stick side.
6. Collect the rebounding ball on the forehand behind the opponent and dribble on.

b) Passing an opponent on the reverse stick using the sideboards, dribbling

1. Dribble the ball in front of the body.
2. The stick forms a 45° angle to the ground.
3. Place the stick, holding it in the reverse stick position, to the left side of the ball with the flat side of the stick pointing to the right; the stick head points to the ground.
4. Push pass the ball firmly against the sideboard to the right (reverse stick side of the opponent).
5. By a fast kick off, go round the opponent on his forehand side.
6. Collect the rebounding ball on the reverse stick behind the opponent and dribble on.

111

5. Incorrect movements

Passing an opponent using the sideboards

1. The ball is played against the sideboard either too near or too far away from the opponent; the opponent can gather the ball.
2. The ball hits the sideboard at too wide an angle; it bounces back too early so that the opponent can gather it up.
3. The ball hits the sideboard at too sharp an angle; spin is created and it runs away close to and along the sideboard.
4. The ball does not bounce back sufficiently fast enough.

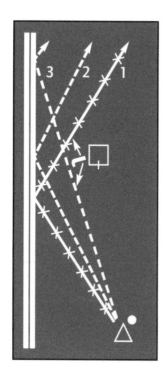

6. Corrective measures

Passing an opponent using the sideboards

1. Pick your eyes up from the ball so that you can watch the opponent and judge your distance from him accurately.
2. Narrow the stroke angle.
3. Make the stroke angle larger.
4. Push pass the ball harder at the sideboard; increase the impact.

7. The rules

1. In indoor hockey you are allowed to bounce the ball off the sideboards. (I).
2. You can supplement a player on your side by using the sideboard. (I).
3. If when you play the ball it jumps over the sideboard and goes out of play, the opponent brings the ball back into play by hitting back into play at a point 1 m away from the sideboard exactly where it went out. If the ball goes out off a defender over the sideboard within the shooting circle, it is brought back into play from in front of the shooting circle. (I).

8. The laws

The sideboards

The sidelines in indoor hockey are marked using the sideboards, which are 10 cm square. Their side inclination to the playing area is 1 cm = 10%.

The goal dead ball line has no sideboards laid down.

2.4.4 Three-zone Exercise

1. The game

The game is played with a 2:3 attack minority. The playing area is divided into 3 equal sized zones. A defender (x) may not leave his defensive one third area. Thus the minority is maintained (at 2:3). The defending team gains the majority from the middle third so that they can disrupt the build up of the attack early enough. Goals may only be scored from the goal shooting zone. No goalkeeper is assigned.

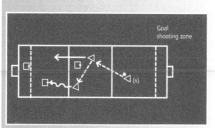

2. Tactics

a) Attack

Each attack phase begins by bringing the ball under control in one's own half. Watch out that the distance between the defenders and the sideboards does not get too narrow. In indoor hockey don't allow yourself to be pushed too close to the sideboards/sideline.

b) Defence

By using a lunge step you can increase your defensive capabilities, being able to defend quickly and without any great deal of preparation. The attacker doesn't recognise the defence tactic until later on. Tackle firmly; hesitation gives your intentions away to the attacker. Always position yourself between the attacker and your own goal. Try to close with the opponent as he is receiving the ball and try to disrupt his play. Block the path of the ball by trying to reach out towards the sideboard with your stick.

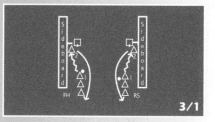

3. Techniques

Simple defence actions using the stick held low

1. Simple defence actions using the stick held low/ lunge step and the sideboard

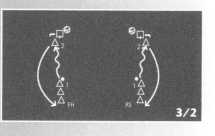

on the forehand, or reverse stick against a semi-active stationary defender; the attacker runs to the start position again.

2. Simple defence actions using the stick held low and lunge step on the forehand, or reverse stick against a semi-active stationary defender; the attacker runs to the start position again.

3. Simple defence actions using the stick held low and lunge step with a rapid change of defence position (180° turn); the defender is semi-active; defence is done on the forehand or reverse stick; the attacker runs one after the other at the defender.

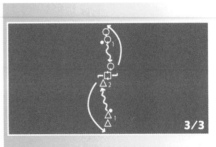

3/3

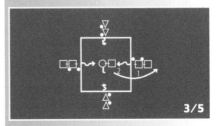

3/4

4. The Dragon's Cave

Four 'Dragons' are standing in their caves (squares) with one foot on a ball, from which they may not move. The attackers have to make their way through the caves. The Dragons have to capture the ball by simple forehand or reverse stick defensive actions. Attackers who complete going through the caves go back to the start. After certain periods the teams change roles. *Which team can capture the ball most often?*

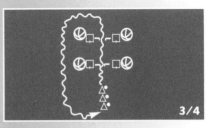

3/5

5. Quick turnovers

The players stand, as illustrated, on the sides of a square, in the middle of which there is a defender. The attackers play round the defenders in the square in a particular order 1-2-3-4 or 1-3-2-4 and so on. The defender tries to prevent this. If the defender is successful, the attacker returns to the start; otherwise he lines up on the opposite side. *Which defender manages the most successes?*

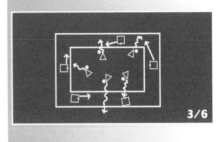

3/6

6. Freeing game
One team stands in the inner playing area with the other in the outer. The team in the inner playing area has to try to break out through the other playing area with the ball, while the other team tries to prevent them from doing this. Each lost ball means the end of the break out for the individual player. After a laid down time the teams change over areas. *Which team manages to prevent the most breakouts?*

4. Description of the movements

a) Simple defence action using the forehand stick held low and a lunge step

1. The player stands legs apart facing the attacker with the ball.
2. The knees are slightly bent; weight is on the balls of the feet; arms slightly bent.
3. The stick is held at hip height in front of the body with the flat side facing forward; the stick head points upwards.
4. The left hand holds the stick in the basic position; the right hand lets go of the stick.
5. The stick is held only by the left hand; the left arm is quickly stretched down.
6. At the same time, the left leg lunges forwards and to the right.
7. Bring the stick horizontally to the ground and stop the ball.
8. The flat side of the stick points forwards; the stick head is inclined a little forwards – watch out for the stick angle bent slightly forward to protect the ball (see page 89).
9. Using the stick in a 'swiping' movement to the middle of the body, collect the ball to be able to play on.
10. If the defensive move fails go back into the initial 'ready' position.

b) Simple defence action using the reverse stick held low and a lunge step

1. The player stands legs apart facing the attacker with the ball.

2. Knees are slightly bent; weight is on the balls of the feet; arms slightly bent.

3. The stick is held at hip height in front of the body with the flat side facing forward; the stick head points upwards.

4. The left hand only holds the top of the stick; the right hand lets go of the stick.

5. Bring the left arm to the left and push through firmly, turning the stick into the reverse stick hold.

6. At the same time the right leg lunges forwards and to the left.

7. Bring the stick on to the ground with the stick head pointing downwards and stop the ball.

8. Tip the stick in the direction of the advancing ball; watch out for the protective stick angle and position so that the ball does not run underneath the bend of the stick head.

9. Using the stick in a 'swiping' movement to the middle of the body, collect the ball to be able to play on.

10. If the defensive move fails, go back into the initial 'ready' position.

c) Simple defence action using the forehand stick held low, a lunge step and the sideboard

1. The player stands legs apart facing the attacker with the ball.

2. Knees are slightly bent; weight is on the balls of the feet; arms slightly bent.

3. The stick is held at hip height in front of the body with the flat side facing forward; the stick head points upwards.

4. The left hand holds the stick in the basic position; the right hand lets go of the stick.

5. The stick is held only by the left hand; the left arm is quickly stretched down.

6. At the same time, one leg lunges forwards and to the right.

7. Bring the stick horizontally to the ground and at the same time touch the sideboard with it in order to stop the ball.

8. The flat side of the stick points forwards; the stick head is inclined a little forwards – watch out for the protective stick angle and position.

9. The stick head must make contact with the sideboard in order to make sure the ball is stopped.

10. Collect the ball and play on.

11. If the defensive move fails, go back into the initial 'ready' position.

d) Simple defence action using the reverse stick held low, a lunge step and the sideboard

1. The player stands legs apart facing the attacker with the ball.
2. Knees are slightly bent; weight is on the balls of the feet; arms slightly bent.
3. The stick is held at hip height in front of the body with the flat side facing forward; the stick head points upwards.
4. The left hand only holds the stick in the turn position and at the top of it; the right hand lets go of the stick.
5. Bring the left arm to the left and push through firmly, turning the stick into the reverse stick hold.
6. At the same time, the right leg lunges forwards and to the left.
7. Bring the stick with the stick head down on to the ground and at the same time touch the sideboard with it in order to stop the ball.
8. Tip the stick in the direction of the advancing ball; watch out for the protective stick angle and position so that the ball does not run underneath the bend of the stick head.
9. The stick head must make contact with the sideboard in order to make sure the ball is stopped.
10. Collect the ball and play on.
11. If the defensive move fails go back into the initial 'ready' position.

5. Incorrect movements

Simple defence action using the forehand / reverse stick held low, a lunge step and the sideboard

1. The left arm is not pushed down enough; too little range.
2. The left leg is not far enough into the lunge step on the forehand.
3. The right leg has not been lunged out enough on the reverse stick.
4. The stick is tipped to the rear on the forehand; flat edge is skewed.
5. On the reverse stick, the left hand is not holding in the turn hold, and the stick cannot be turned enough into the reverse stick hold.
6. On the reverse stick it is not pushed forward enough; the ball runs through under the stick.
7. The stick is not brought close enough to the ground on the forehand and the reverse stick.
8. The stick head has not made contact with the sideboard; the ball can be played through by using the sideboard.
9. The defender runs into the attacker.

6. Corrective measures

Simple defence action using the forehand / reverse stick held low, a lunge step and the sideboard

1. Push the left arm all the way through.
2. Consciously make the step with the left leg.
3. Consciously bring the right leg forward.
4. Adopt a protective position over the ball with the stick; tip the stick head further forward.

5. Turn the back of your left hand more upwards.
6. Turn the stick more deliberately into the direction of the advancing ball.
7. Move the stick over the ground so that your knuckles feel contact with the ground.
8. Take a bigger lunge step in order to make contact with the sideboard.
9. As a defender, be ready for the attacker and watch him carefully – he will have the ball under control and will have you in his field of vision.

7. The rules

1. For a foul outside the shooting circle you will be awarded a free hit on the spot where the foul was made on you. (FP/MH).
2. For a foul against you as a defender inside the shooting circle you can take the free hit from anywhere inside the shooting circle or up to 16 yards (14.63 m) in front of your own goal line at the point where the foul was made. (FP/MH).
3. For a foul against you outside the shooting circle you take a free push shot at the spot where the foul was made on you. (I).
4. For a foul against you as a defender inside the shooting circle you can take the free push shot from anywhere inside the shooting circle. (I).
5. When carrying out a free push hit the opponent may not be nearer than 3m to the ball. (I).
6. For an intentional foul inside the shooting circle a penalty flick is awarded.
7. Any infringement may be penalised by both being sent off the field and a personal penalty awarded.

8. The laws

Warnings – Being sent off

1. Warning for incorrect behaviour (green card).
2. A sending off (for remainder of the game) occurs following a second warning (yellow card).
3. Sent off to the 'sin-bin' for 2-5 minutes (indoor hockey) and 5-15 minutes (outdoor hockey) is awarded for rough play or answering back at the umpire.
4. The time must be given to the timekeeper. The player may not be told for how long.
5. Sent off for the remainder of the game (2 yellow cards = automatic red card).
6. In a match a player may be substituted after 10 minutes (for adults) or 7 minutes (youths).

2.4.5 Game with Reversed Goals

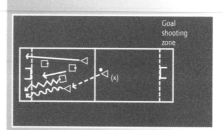

1. The game

The game is played with a 2:3 attack minority. The goals are placed forward on the goal shooting zone line but with their goal mouths pointing towards the rear goal line (see illustration). No team has an assigned goalkeeper. The defenders have to try to disrupt the build up of the opponent's play by at least the centre line. The attackers must try, as far as possible, to storm towards the goal line in order to score a goal from there. One attacker (x) stays in his own half in order to maintain a minority in the opponent's defence.

2. Tactics

a) Attack

Anticipate what the defence will do and play through at the right moment. Create fresh possibilities to receive the ball by moving around constantly. Take care not to cause an obstruction.

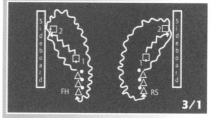

b) Defence

Don't go into the attack straight away if you have time, but try to distract your opponent. Keep up with the attacker and wait for him to make a mistake. As you follow your opponent, wait for the moment when the ball is not covered by the stick. When confronted with a strong 'dribbler', covering and marking him is the best form of defence. Play the ball from the inside to the outside (away from the goal). Push the opponent into an unfavourable shooting position away from the goal to the sideline.

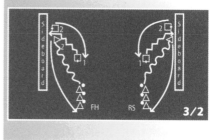

3. Techniques

Covering and Marking in defence

1. Straight forward covering and marking of the attacker by the defender using a stick dummy in both the forehand and reverse stick positions. Return to the start.
2. Straight forward covering and marking of the attacker by defensive use of the sideboards in both the forehand and reverse stick positions. Return to the start.
3. Covering and marking defensive play using the stick in a limited area. Run back to the original position.

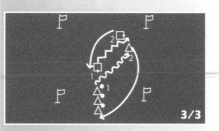

3/3

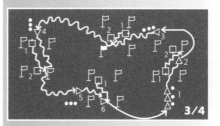

3/4

4. The Sweat Boxes

A defender stands in each of the 'box' areas. He has to try to prevent an attacker taking his ball through his box area on to the next one. The attacker has to go through all the boxes. If the defender is successful in preventing his box being crossed, the attacker takes a further ball and plays on. Changeover. *Which team manages to defend their box areas the most successfully?*

3/5

5. Calling the Month

The players line up on the narrow side of the playing area; the defender stands in front of the centre line (as seen from the other players). The defender calls the name of a month. All the players who were born in the month called out, cross over to the other side. The defender tries to take the ball off them. Because there will only be a few players crossing at any one time there is an opportunity to employ covering and marking defensive play. *Which defender manages to collect the most balls?*

3/6

6. Robbing the ball

The corners of the playing area are marked off as 'safes'. Two teams try to rob the ball from their opponent's safes in order to take it to their safes; at the same time they try to defend the balls in their own safes. Every player may attack the opponent's safes. On the way back the ball has to be wrested from him and brought under control of the defender, who dribbles it back to his safe. Which team loses the least number of balls?

4. Description of the movements

a) Covering and marking in defence – forehand

1. The defender stands legs apart facing the attacker with the ball. Knees are slightly bent; weight is on the balls of the feet.
2. The arms are slightly bent. The stick is held at hip height with the flat side facing forward; the stick head points upwards.
3. Take the right leg backwards; the left hand holds the top of the stick; the right lets go of the stick.
4. The left shoulder points towards the advancing opponent; hold the stick sideways to the rear.
5. Covering and marking, run sideways and backwards; wait for an attack opportunity; at the same time bring the stick in front of the body.
6. Attack the attacker on the forehand on the side where he is dribbling the ball; get slightly in front of the attacker, overtaking him.
7. Go for the ball if it is temporarily not under control.
8. The right hand grasps the stick as for the forehand stop.

9. Rapid lunge forwards; left foot forward.
10. Bend both knees.
11. Switch your weight on to the front leg.
12. Bend the upper body.
13. Lay the stick down on the ground like a 'plank'; watch out for the protective stick angle and position.
14. Stop the ball with the whole length of the stick.
15. After gaining possession of the ball, bring it under control and play on.

b) Covering and marking in defence – reverse stick

1. The defender stands legs apart facing the attacker with the ball. Knees are slightly bent; weight is on the balls of the feet.
2. The arms are slightly bent. The stick is held at hip height with the flat side facing forward; the stick head points upwards.
3. Take the left leg backwards; both hands hold the stick.

4. The defender anticipates the attacker with his right shoulder pointing towards the advancing opponent.
5. Covering and marking, run sideways and backwards; wait for an attack opportunity; start to overtake the attacker a little.
6. Let go of the stick with the right hand; the left hand holds the top of the stick.

7. Bring the stick in front of the body in the reverse stick hold; the stick head points towards the ground.
8. Attack the ball with the reverse stick; the attacker is dribbling the ball on his right hand side.
9. Wait for the moment when the attacker is not covering the ball.

10. The right hand grasps the stick as for the reverse stick stop.
11. Rapid lunge forwards; right foot forward.
12. Bend both knees.
13. Switch your weight on to the front leg.
14. Bend the upper body.
15. Stretch both arms out.
16. Lay the stick down on the ground like a 'plank'; watch out for the protective stick angle and position.
17. Stop the ball with the whole length of the stick.
18. After gaining possession of the ball, bring it under control and play on.

5. Incorrect movements

Covering and marking in defence – forehand/reverse stick

1. The defender runs into the attacker who can play round him.
2. The defender doesn't wait during the marking phase and attacks too hastily.
3. The defender does not let go of the stick with the right hand.
4. In defence the wrong leg is placed forward; on the forehand – the right leg; on the reverse stick – the left one.
5. The ball runs away under the stick.
6. On the defensive reverse stick the ball runs under the stick head.
7. Weight is not placed on the forward leg; leg not placed firmly down enough; lack of pressure on the stick.
8. After taking possession of the ball from the opponent the defender creates an obstruction.

6. Corrective measures

Covering and marking in defence – forehand/reverse stick

1. Wait patiently for the attacker to come on.
2. Run alongside, covering and marking without attacking the ball.
3. In the defence the stick is only held at the top of it by the left hand.
4. Always bring the leg on the side of the attacker forward; on the forehand – the left one, and reverse stick – the right one.
5. Press the stick on to the ground like a 'plank'.
6. Make a more protective stick angle.
7. Consciously switch your weight on to the forward leg.
8. Watch out for your position with the ball relative to the attacker; the ball must always be playable by the attacker and yourself.

7. The rules

You may attack an opponent from the left-hand side providing that you play the ball without obstructing the opponent's body or his stick. (FP/MH/I).

8. The laws

Unsporting behaviour

The umpire may take measures against unsporting behaviour by either the player or the trainer to ensure that the game progresses in a sporting way.

2.4.6 Goal Shooting by Numbers

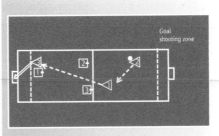

1. The game

The players of each team are given an ascending number. Each team member has to score a goal in a number order which has been worked out before the game and kept secret from the opponents. The exercise leader is given the order of goal scorers beforehand. Each team has to play freely until the next one in the order has scored a goal. Goals must be scored from within a goal shooting zone. There is no fixed goalkeeper assigned.

2. Tactics

a) Attack

Vary the passes; the attacker will soon recognise a repeated pattern of play. Note the position of the opponents in relation to your own players; your passing actions will be according to how they stand. Pass to the best-placed player on your side. Try to bring your outside players into the game by long passes. When passing take note of the field conditions. Use indirect passes off the sideboards (I).

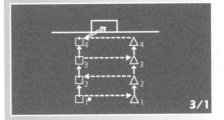

b) Defence

Use a combination of different passes (diagonal/oblique/through passes). If the opponent is not accurate with his passing you can easily disrupt his play. From a defensive position you will have a good overview of the game; watch out for through passes and passing in uncovered areas. Avoid passing diagonally across your own goal mouth, as well as passing back to your own goalkeeper.

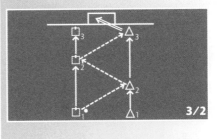

3. Techniques

Passing variations with a shot at goal

1. Forehand and reverse stick diagonal pass and collecting up the ball (cross-over of the forehand/reverse stick pick up), dribbling and shot at goal. Changeover sides.

2. Oblique pass on the forehand and reverse stick and collecting up the ball, dribbling and shot at goal; also an oblique pass as a direct passing movement.

3. Through pass followed by a shot at goal.

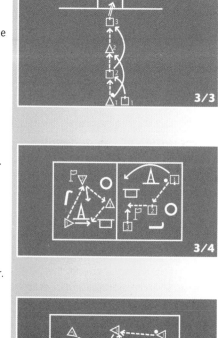

3/3

4. Passing by numbers with obstacles

The playing area is divided into two equal halves. There are the same numbers of players and obstacles in each half. The players, who all have a number assigned to them, pass the ball in a predetermined order. Each player must keep on the move. *Which team manages to go through 1,2,3...goes first?*

3/4

5. Passing by numbers with defence disruption

Each player gets a number assigned to him. All the players move freely round the area. In a predetermined number order each player receives the ball. The defender, who does not know the predetermined number order, tries to disrupt play. If he is successful, he changes numbers with the player who last gave the pass. *Which pass always finds its target?*

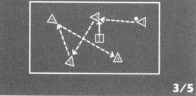

3/5

6. No-man's-land

The playing area is divided into three zones as illustrated. Two attackers and a defender

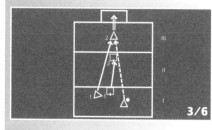

3/6

stand opposite each other in the first zone. The player with the ball pushes a through pass into the third zone. The second attacker tries to collect the pass. The defender may not attack in the no-man's-land (2nd zone). The defence as well as the shot at goal occurs in the third zone. *Which attacker manages to complete the most collected push passes?*

4. Description of the movements
Diagonal/oblique and through passes

1. Diagonal pass: playing on to another team member who is positioned to the side of the player with the ball.
2. Oblique pass: playing on to another team member as he runs to collect.
3. Through pass: playing the ball so that it takes the shortest way towards the goal; the attacker has to move rapidly after the ball in order to collect it; the speed of the ball must be judged well.

5. Incorrect movements
Diagonal/oblique and through passes

1. The ball ends up behind your team member because he is moving forwards.
2. Your team member cannot reach the ball.
3. The pass was not through enough; it becomes an oblique pass rather than a through one.
4. The opponent intercepts the ball.

6. Corrective measures
Diagonal/oblique and through passes

1. Play the ball diagonally forward into the path of the running team member; remember that your team member is

running to get forward.
2. Serve the ball up more accurately; judge the speed of your team member better.

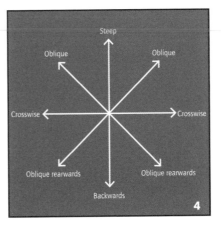

The path of the ball when passing

3. Play the ball on its shortest path towards the goal.
4. Watch what your opponent is doing in his position before you pass; give your pass more impetus if necessary.

7. The rules

1. In outdoor hockey as well as indoor hockey there is **no** offside rule.

2.5 Game Situation 5 Correct Play – Attacking/ Defending

2.5.1 Games Using the Shooting Circle without a Goalkeeper

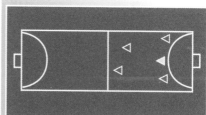

Small field 3:2-System

1. The game

The game is played on the pitch with the shooting circle being used for the first time. Goals may only be scored when shot from within the shooting circle. Neither team has a goalkeeper assigned.

2. Tactics

a) Attack

Use the flick to score a goal; using this shot you can place the ball high up into the goal. Using the flick you can pass to a player positioned some distance away. Only use the flick when you are sure you will not endanger another player.

b) Defence

Take care: a well-executed flick can surprise a defence that has moved forward. Decide amongst your own team what position each will take up for such a move. Be careful when covering and marking that an obstruction infringement is not created.

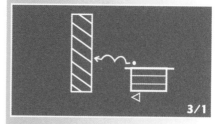

3. Techniques

The flick

1. Do the flick with the hand (without a stick) against the wall off a tall box (use the arm in place of the stick).

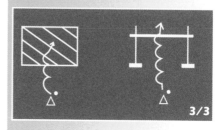

128

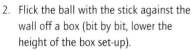

2. Flick the ball with the stick against the wall off a box (bit by bit, lower the height of the box set-up).
3. Flick the ball off the ground against a wall/ into an open space/ over an obstacle (e.g., high jump poles).

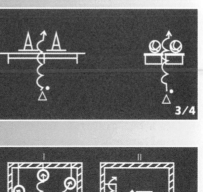

4. Flicking through a gap

Several groups organise a game of flicking through gaps – over a bench/ little boxes/ built up larger box arrangement etc., with skittles/ marker flags/ balls etc....*Which team manage to flick the most balls through the gaps?*

5. Flicking at targets

Two teams carry out flick shots at a goal. Hoops are hanging at different heights in the goal mouth; or you can have an arrangement of small and large boxes built up in the goal mouth. The aim is to flick the ball through: I – the hoops or II – into the goal. *Which team manages to get the most goals?*

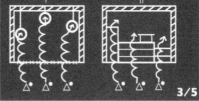

6. How many 'lives'?

Two groups carry out flick shots at a goal e.g., at the upper right corner or the bottom left from 10 different positions (10 'lives'). If a player misses a goal he loses a 'life'. *Which team ends up with the most lives?*

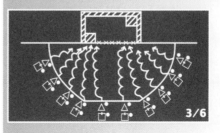

4. Description of the movements

a) Forehand standing flick with a stationary ball

1. The left shoulder points in the direction that you wish the ball to travel.
2. The feet are positioned in a slightly straddled stance at right angles to the direction of the flick; the knees are slightly bent.
3. The left hand grasps the top of the stick in the basic position (with the back of the hand pointing in the direction of the flick).
4. The right hand grasps the stick on the grip about two hand widths below the left one (with the back of it pointing away from the direction of the flick).
5. The left lower arm forms an approximate straight line with the stick.
6. The ball lies approximately 1.5 feet in front of the left foot.
7. The stick head lies inclined underneath the ball; the stick is prominently inclined backwards.
8. The body weight is switched onto the rear (right) leg.
9. The right shoulder is dipped considerably lower than the left one.
10. Switch the body weight rapidly onto the front (left) leg
11. Bring the right hand forward rapidly.
12. The left hand presses firmly down on the top end of the stick (distinct tipping movement – the right hand comes in front of the left one).
13. The ball lifts up sharply.
14. The stick follows through in a straight line behind the ball; at the end of the

A

B

movement the stick head is pointing upwards.

15. Don't bring the stick above the height of the shoulders (infringement of the rules).

The movement is conducted from low down from behind to forwards and upwards; the speed of the tipping movement governs the speed and the force of the ball; the height of the ball is governed by how deep the body weight is in the movement.

b) Practising for the flick

1. The player stands next to a large box with his left shoulder pointing in the direction of the flick.
2. The ball lies on the front edge of the box.
3. Bring the hand underneath the rear side of the ball (representing the stick).
4. Switching the body weight from the rear to front and stretching out the arm (representing the stick) 'flick' the ball.
5. Compare the description of the movements as above.

C

D

131

5. Incorrect movements

Forehand standing flick with a stationary ball

1. The stick head is not positioned under the ball; the ball cannot be lifted up.
2. The stick head is not close to the ball.
3. The stick is inclined too sharply; the ball jumps over the stick head.
4. The ball doesn't lie in front of the left foot.
5. The ball is too far away from the body/too near the body.
6. At the beginning of the movement the body weight is not on the rear leg.
7. The tipping motion is too slow.
8. The hands are too far apart; a tipping motion isn't possible.
9. The hands are too close together; insufficient fulcrum; too much effort needed.
10. The tipping motion is not controlled; the stick head goes over shoulder height.

6. Corrective measures

Forehand standing flick with a stationary ball

1. Incline the stick more to the rear.
2. Place the stick head directly behind the ball; you should not hear the stick making contact with the ball.
3. Place the stick in a steeper position.
4. Place the ball on a level with the left foot.
5. Place the ball away from the body at a distance, which makes the stick form a 45° angle with the ground.
6. Pull the right shoulder further backwards.
7. Practice pushing more firmly down on the top end of the stick.

8. Place the hands closer together so that they are two hand widths apart.
9. Place the hands further apart so that they are two hand widths apart.
10. Control the stick better.

7. The rules

1. You may use the flick to shoot at goal from within the shooting circle (FP/MH/I).
2. You may also use the flick for a penalty stroke shot. However you can only take one pace to take the shot (FP/MH/I).
3. You are allowed to use the flick to pass the ball providing you do not endanger another player (FP/MH).

8. The laws

The shooting circle (also called the 'D')

In hockey the shooting circle plays an important role. Goals can only be scored if the shot is taken from within the shooting circle, or the ball rebounds/is deflected off another attacking player inside the shooting circle. Infringements by the defending team are punished by the award of a short corner/penalty or even a penalty stroke.

2.5.2 Games with a Goal-keeper - Part 1

1. The game

For the first time a proper game is played with a team in accordance with the rules and proper goal scoring. All the rules are applicable less the penalty corner. Infringements in the shooting circle are penalised by awarding a free hit against the opponent outside the shooting circle.

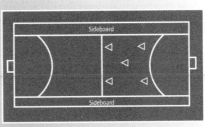

Abb 3 2:1:2-System

2. Tactics

a) Attack

As the goalkeeper note where your own unmarked players are; the build up to a new attack starts each time the ball comes back into play. Play on to your own players so that they can receive the ball without any danger.

b) Defence

As the goalkeeper watch out for the attackers and not just only for the player with the ball. Don't stand too far in front of the goal line; the ball can be flicked over you into the goal. Position yourself in relation to the ball so that you always halve the angle of attack. Don't stand rooted to the spot, move around following the play.

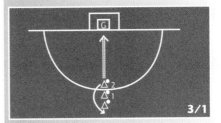

3. Techniques

Goalkeeper training I

1. Basic goalkeeping position on the goal line: defending by kicking with the boots, pads and stick.
2. Basic goalkeeping position on the goal line: defending by using the body and hands; change stick holding hand to effect defence if a glove is being used – nowadays it is quite usual that the one glove has a flat palm board, which the

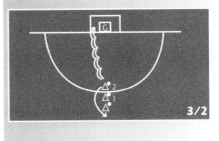

133

goalkeeper uses to deflect the ball away. Players use the flick shot.

3. Goalkeeper positional play in the goal: Goalkeeper covers the narrow angle. Players push in or hit/flick the shots all from the left side then from the right side. Players push in or hit/flick shots alternately from the left and then the right side.

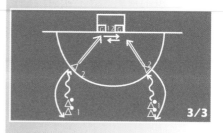

4. Goalkeeper positional play in the goal
The goalkeeper changes his position according to what the attackers are doing. The shooting position and angle is left to the players themselves. The players shoot at goal one after the other; first from the left hand side and then from the right hand.

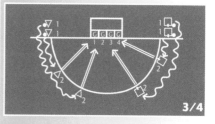

5. Reaction training for the goalkeeper on the goal line
The goalkeeper stands on the goal line with his back to the other players. Players push in or hit/flick the shots – all from different positions at the goal. The time between shots is made shorter as play progresses. The strength of the shots becomes gradually harder. **N.B.** The players give an acoustic signal to the goalkeeper just as they are about to shoot so that the goalie can turn around quick enough.

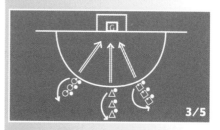

6. Reaction training for the goalkeeper on the goal line
The goalkeeper stands on the goal line and looks at the attacking player. The attacker runs through a soft mat or round boxes so that his approach is hidden from the goalkeeper. Once the attacker emerges from behind the obstacle he shoots at goal. The route round the obstacle can be left for the attacker to decide. The timing between shots is made shorter.

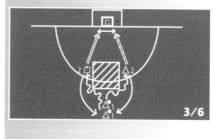

4. Description of the movements

a) Goalkeeper positioned to be able to defend the shot

1. Lower region: use kickers/pads
2. Middle region: use stick/hand/body
3. Upper region: use hand

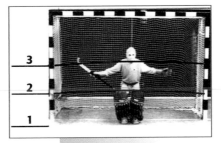

b) Goalkeeper in the ready position

1. Feet are slightly apart; the ankles are lifted up slightly; weight is on the balls of the feet.
2. Knees, hip joints and elbows are slightly bent.
3. The right hand grasps the stick in the middle; the flat side is pointing forwards.
4. The left hand is open with the palm showing to the front.

c) Goalkeeper defends using:

1. *Kickers*
   a) Kick away with the tip of the kicker; used to ward off danger.
   b) Kick away with the inside of the kicker; used to defend and pass over a short distance.
2. *Pads*
   a) Pads should be facing forwards and slightly inclined to deflect the ball down onto the ground.
   b) With the pads sideways (with the feet slightly apart the leg is turned outwards and stretched out).

135

3. *The stick*

   a) Using the flat side of the stick pointing forward defend up to shoulder height; don't hit the ball back into the field of play.

4. *The hand*

   a) For the ball above shoulder height – on the stick side as well – defend with the hand.

   b) For every ball above knee height – on the glove hand side.

   c) Let the ball simply rebound off the hand; striking the ball with the hand or holding it is not allowed.

5. Incorrect movements

Defence by the goalkeeper

1. The goalkeeper kicks the ball high back into play (Indoor).
2. The ball bounces high off the pads back into play, the pads are not inclined.
3. The goalkeeper hits the ball back into play with the stick.
4. The goalkeeper hits the ball away with the hand.
5. The goalkeeper holds the ball with the hand in the air or down on the ground.
6. The goalkeeper wards off the ball straight into the field of play; gives a chance for another shot at goal.

6. Corrective measures

Defence by the goalkeeper

1. Do a follow through swing with the kicking foot and body; the tip of the foot points towards the ground.
2. Incline the pads forwards and downwards so that they form a sharp angle with the ground.
3. Merely let the ball drop off the stick; push pass or kick the ball away to the side.
4. Simply let the ball drop off the hand onto the ground; then kick or push pass with the stick away to the side.
5. See Number 4 above.
6. Ward the ball off towards the side line.

7. The rules

1. The goalkeeper may stop the ball and kick it away with the foot, or play it with the stick. (FP/MH/I).
2. The goalkeeper may not catch the ball, throw it with hand or cover it with the hand. (FP/MH/I).
3. You may not endanger your opponent when clearing the ball rapidly i.e., kicking high. (FP/MH).
4. In indoor hockey you may only kick the ball away.

8. The laws

Goalkeeping equipment

1. Kickers (worn over boots)
2. Goalkeeping pads
3. Abdominal protector
4. Chest protector
5. Goalkeeping gloves
6. Helmet
7. Face mask (as part of helmet)
8. Stick

See illustrations on Page 97

2.5.3 Games with a Goal-keeper - Part 2

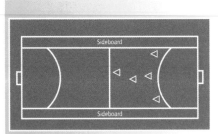

Indoor 3:1:1-System

1. The game

The game is played in the same way as the game in Chapter 2.5.2 (p.133).

2. Tactics

a) Attack

As the goalkeeper, clear the ball in such a way that it goes to one of your own players. In indoor hockey, clear the ball in such a way that it rebounds off the sideboards to one of your own players. Always try to clear the ball off to one side. Be able to mark balls shot from outside the shooting circle in case they rebound off the goal posts – this gives the opponent a chance to shoot a goal with a ball that has rebounded.

b) Defence

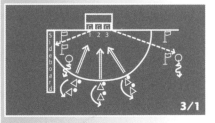

3/1

Come out from your goal resolutely and with determination. By coming out cleverly and skilfully from your goal, you can make the opponent have to choose a poor attack angle relative to the goal mouth. You may not hold on to the ball as a goalkeeper; this causes follow-up chances for the attacker. As far as possible clear the ball off towards the side. Be alert to balls shot from outside the shooting circle in case they rebound off the goal posts – this gives the attacker a chance to shoot a goal with a ball that has rebounded.

3. Techniques

Goalkeeper training II

1. Goalkeeper defends his goal line with players shooting at him. The goalkeeper clears the ball by kicking off the line in

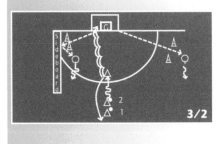

3/2

such a way that the ball goes through a
gate formed by marker flags to a player
on his own side who begins to mount a
counter-attack. In indoor hockey, clear
the ball via the sideboards to a player on
your own side. The player shoots at goal.

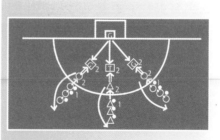

2. Goalkeeper defends his goal line with
   players shooting at him. The goalkeeper
   clears the ball as above but now using
   his glove, stick, body or pads. The players
   shoot or flick at the goal.
3. The goalkeeper runs out to narrow the
   angle to the disadvantage of the
   attacker; the goalkeeper clears using his
   body, kickers or stick

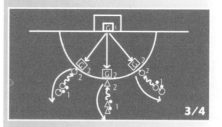

*4. Goalkeeper runs out to narrow attack
angle*

The goalkeeper runs out as far as the edge of
the shooting circle line in order to narrow the
attack angle; in any case the attacker cannot
score a goal if he shoots from outside the
shooting circle. The players shoot from a
variety of positions.

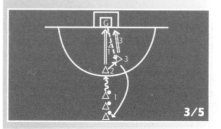

*5. Reaction of the goalkeeper to a follow-up
shot*

The goalkeeper clears the ball off the line
back into play; the attacker follows up and
tries to score a goal from the rebound.

*6. Reaction of the goalkeeper to a follow-up
shot*

The player runs into the shooting circle and
shoots at goal. The goalie clears the ball
back into play. Player 'o' also has a ball and
immediately shoots. Shooting positions are
changed around.

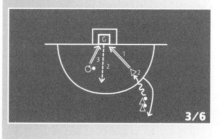

4. Description of the movements

a) Goalkeeper positions

1. The goalkeeper stands on an imaginary line bisecting the angle.
2. The sides of the angle are formed by lines to the goal posts.
3. If the attacker runs at the goal from the side, the goalkeeper stands on that side of the goal; he is covering the 'near' corner.
4. The goalkeeper stands in such a position so that he can prevent a goal by using the least amount of defensive movements.

b) Running out to narrow the angle

1. The position of the goalkeeper is not always dependent on the position of the striker but also how far he is away from the goal.
2. If a player attacks on his own, the goalkeeper should move out towards him in order to narrow the shot angle.
3. The goalkeeper can increase his defence by lunging forwards; the lunge takes place moving forward to one side diagonally; in this way he covers and narrows the attack angle even more.
4. The goalkeeper throws himself sideways into the path of the attacker so that he can cover the ball with the whole of the side of his body. The goalkeeper can thus effectively cover a large amount of the goal area.
5. The goalkeeper tries to block the attacker as far forward as the shooting circle line (I).

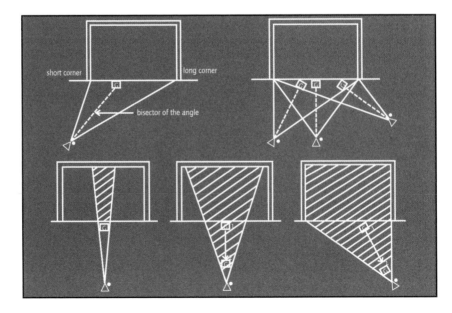

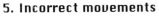

5. Incorrect movements

Goalkeeper positions / running out to narrow attack angle

1. The goalkeeper is not standing in a position that bisects the attack angle.
2. The goalkeeper is not defending the near corner against a side delivered attack.
3. The goalkeeper remains on the goal line; this affords a broad attack angle; good position for the attacker.
4. The lunge takes place parallel to the goal line affording a wide attack angle possibility for the opponent.
5. The goalkeeper moves forward too early and can be easily feinted round.
6. The goalkeeper lets the attacker come forward into the shooting circle; the attacker has a chance at a shot at goal (I).

6. Corrective measures

Goalkeeper positions / running out to narrow attack angle

1. Watch the ball; change your position in the goal mouth accordingly.
2. Place yourself directly next to the goal posts.
3. Come out of the goal resolutely and determined; hesitation increases the striker's chances; narrow the angle so as to cause the opponent to take up a favourable position.
4. Lunge forward diagonally.
5. Stay still for as long as possible in order to anticipate the opponent's intentions.
6. Block the attacker right forward on the edge of the shooting circle (I).

7. The rules

1. The umpire awards a penalty stroke if you have caused an intentional infringement in your own shooting circle or if you prevent the opponents scoring a goal following an intentional infringement caused by you. (FP/MH/I).
2. You may use a push, flick (FP/MH/I), aerial flick (I) to convert a 7 m penalty. The ball may be shot at any height. You may only touch the ball once and may only take one pace when executing the shot. After taking the shot you may not approach either the ball or the goalkeeper.
3. The goalkeeper stands on the goal line (FP/MH/I).
4. All the players in the team must stand behind the nearest 25 m line (FP), outside the shooting circle (MH) or behind the centre line (I).

8. Tips

End of a penalty stroke

A goal is scored when the ball passes over the goal line between the goal posts and underneath the backboard.

If the goalkeeper causes an infringement during the execution of a penalty stroke, even if he has saved the ball, the umpire will award a penalty.

A penalty stroke is declared as ended when the ball comes to a halt inside the shooting circle, or gets stuck in the goalkeeper's pads, or is saved by the goalkeeper, or leaves the shooting circle area (the 'D'). A follow-up shot is not allowed. Play continues by the defending team being allowed to take a free hit (FP/MH) or a free push-in (I).

2.5.4 Playing According to the Rules - Part 1

1. The game

For the first time, the game is played in accordance with the official rules.

2. Tactics

a) Attack

Pass the ball quickly and precisely to the stopper. Push the ball towards the nearest goal post; this is the most direct route. Carry out any corners in a variety of ways; the defence will soon quickly get wise to repeated tactics. Try to play round the goalkeeper if necessary.

b) Defence

The tasks for each defender should have been worked out prior to the game starting.

3. Techniques

Penalty corner – execution

1. Push in through a gap created by e.g., skittles to a stopper who stops the ball (FP/MH/I).
2. Aiming through a gap created by e.g., marker flags, push in, stopping, shot at goal without a goalkeeper.
3. Executing a penalty corner in indoor hockey:

   Variation I.

   Goalkeeper stands in the goal.

   The pusher (1) plays the ball in – the stopper (2) passes the ball on – the striker (4) takes a shot at goal. Prior to the shot at goal the ball must have been stopped correctly by one of the attackers outside the 'D', or have come to a stop, or have touched the stick or the body of a defender.

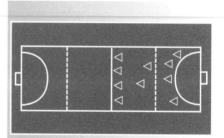

Outdoor Hockey 4:2:4-System

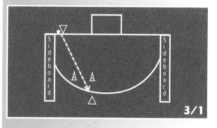

3/1

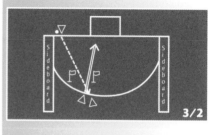

3/2

4. Execution of a penalty corner

Executing a penalty corner in indoor hockey: Variation II.

The pusher (1) plays the ball in – the stopper (2) passes the ball on – the attacker (4) passes the ball on – the pusher (1) runs into the shooting circle and takes a shot at goal. Prior to the shot at goal, the ball must have been stopped correctly by one of the attackers, or have come to a stop, or have touched the stick or the body of a defender.

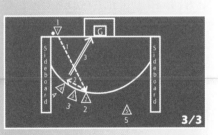

5. Execution of a penalty corner:

Executing a penalty corner in outdoor hockey (full or mini hockey pitch):

Goalkeeper stands in the goal.

The pusher (1) plays the ball into the shooting circle – the stopper (2) runs into the shooting circle, stops the ball and takes a shot at goal.

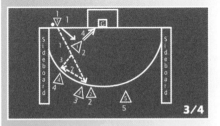

6. Execution of a penalty corner:

Variation I.

Goalkeeper stands in the goal.

Executing a penalty corner in outdoor hockey (full or mini hockey pitch):

The pusher (1) plays the ball into the shooting circle – the stopper (2) runs into the shooting circle and passes the ball on – the pusher (1) runs into the shooting circle and takes a shot at goal. Prior to the shot at goal, the ball must have been stopped still by one of the attackers.

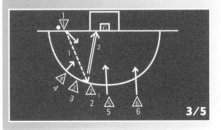

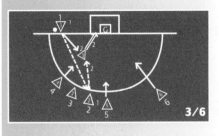

Correct Play – Attacking/Defending

4. Description of the movements

a) Executing a penalty corner – Indoor hockey

1. The pusher stands on the goal line at least 6 m away from goal posts; the team taking the corner may choose from which side of the goal posts the shot will be taken (it is best to use the attacking left side).
2. The pusher-in must have at least one foot on the ground completely off the pitch; one foot may be placed inside the shooting circle.
3. The stopper, the striker and the remainder of the players of the attacking team stand outside the shooting circle with their sticks.
4. The stopper stands on a level with the goal post nearest to the pusher-in.
5. The striker is positioned between the stopper and the sideboard next to the stopper.
6. Following the push-in the stopper and the striker run one or two paces to the ball inside the shooting circle.
7. The stopper stops the ball dead.
8. The striker shoots or flicks at goal.
9. Simultaneously all the attackers run into the shooting circle.
10. The players behind act as 'long-stops' for any missed balls, in order to prevent a rapid counter-attack by the defending team.

144

c) Executing a penalty corner – Outdoor hockey

1. The penalty taker stands at least 9.14 m (10 yards) away from the goal posts on a point on the goal line; the team taking the corner may choose from which side of the goal posts the shot will be taken (it is best to use the attacking left side).
2. The penalty taker must have at least one foot outside the shooting circle; one foot may be placed inside the shooting circle.
3. The remainder of the players of the attacking team stand inside the pitch and outside the shooting circle with their sticks.
4. The penalty taker pushes or hits the ball into the shooting circle; he may not intentionally pitch the ball up into the air.
5. The striker runs about 3 m into the shooting circle.
6. The striker stops the ball dead and shoots straight away at the goal. The shot cannot go higher than the backboard, which is 46 cm high either hitting it or pushing it in.
7. At the same time, the remainder of the players run into the shooting circle in order to gather up any badly defended deflected balls for a second shot at goal.
8. The 'long-stop' stands behind the striker to stop a ball that springs up.
9. The long-stop pushes forward immediately into the shooting circle to shoot at goal.

N.B. Each team has to perfect more than one penalty corner.

145

5. Incorrect movements

Executing a penalty corner

1. Inaccuracy in playing the ball to the stopper in the shooting circle.
2. The stopper lets the ball run through under the stick.
3. The striker fails to stop the ball.
4. The ball is not stopped dead.
5. The ball is struck at the goal so that it rises higher than 46 cm.
6. The attackers don't follow up, poorly defended deflected balls are not exploited to carry out a follow-up shot.

6. Corrective measures

Executing a penalty corner

1. Repeated practice at pushing in through a narrow gap in order to improve target accuracy.
2. Place the stick firmly on the ground.
3. Correct the protective posture of the stick over the ball and stick; cushion the ball in order to reduce its impact.
4. See Number 3.
5. Hit the ball flatter; if necessary practice doing it under a stretched out rope.
6. Everyone, except the long stop, run into the shooting circle as the ball is pushed in.

7. The rules

1. You cause a penalty corner to be awarded, if, as a defender, you cause an infringement in your own shooting circle. (FP/MH/I).
2. A penalty corner will also be awarded if you intentionally hit or push the ball over your own dead line. (FP/MH/I).
3. The umpire will also award a penalty corner if an intentional infringement is committed inside the 25 m line (in outdoor hockey) or in your own half (MH/I).
4. Prior to shooting at goal the ball has to be stopped dead outside the shooting circle, or it must come to a rest by itself. (FP/MH/I).
5. The ball must be stopped so that it is stationary or nearly stationary; it may not move more than 10 cm away from the stick. (FP/MH/I).

8. Tips

Executing a penalty corner

The team carrying out the penalty corner decides from which side the penalty corner will be taken.

The umpire does not blow his whistle to allow the penalty corner to be taken. As soon as the ball leaves the stick head of the striker, the attackers can move into the shooting circle. If the attackers run into the shooting circle too early, the umpire can demand that the corner be taken again. If the defenders are disadvantaged he can give a free hit or push out for the defending team. The same applies if the attackers repeatedly commit an infringement. The pusher cannot score a goal directly. No other player – besides the pusher – can stand nearer than 3 m (indoor hockey) or 5 m (FP/MH) to the ball.

146

2.5.5 Playing According to the Rules - Part 2

1. The game

Once again, the game follows the normal official rules.

2. Tactics

a) Attack

The tasks of each of the team members should be decided prior to the game starting.

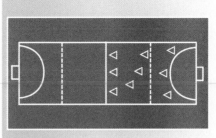

Outdoor Hockey 1:3:3:3-System with sweeper

b) Defence

Decide amongst yourselves whether the goalkeeper plays behind the defence cover or in front of it. Let your fastest defender run to mark the stopper or striker. Two players assist in securing the goal mouth area.

3. Techniques

Penalty corner – defence

1. Defence against a penalty corner with a goalkeeper, pusher, stopper and striker. (Indoor hockey). The goalkeeper remains in the goal mouth – defender (1) runs out at the stopper and striker.

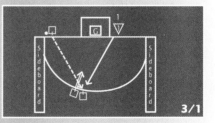

2. Defence against a penalty corner with a goalkeeper and three defenders with a pusher, stopper and striker. (Indoor hockey). The goalkeeper takes one pace forward of the goal – defender (4) runs behind the goalkeeper into the goal mouth to secure the narrow corner and to mark and cover the pusher – defender (5) moves into the long corner of the goal to cover there.

3. Defending against the penalty corner as a standard situation with the goalkeeper behind the backs (defenders). The goalkeeper takes one pace forward of the

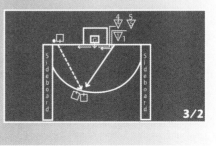

goal – defender (1) runs at the stopper
and the striker – defender (2) runs at the
attacker (A) – defender (4) runs behind
the goalkeeper into the narrow corner –
defender (5) runs into the long corner –
defender (3) runs into the shooting circle
in order to ward off any eventual quick
counter-attack.

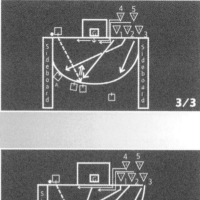

3/3

4. Penalty corner – Defence

Defending against the penalty corner as a
standard situation with the goalkeeper in
front of the backs (defenders) (indoor hockey).
The goalkeeper runs out of the goal at the
stopper and the striker – defender (1) runs at
the attacker (A) – defender (2) runs at the
stopper – defender (4) runs into the near
corner next to the goal post to cover and
block any eventual push in shot – defender
(5) runs into the goal to cover it – defender
(3) runs into the shooting circle in order to
ward off any eventual quick counter-attack.

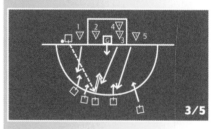

3/4

5. Penalty corner – Defence

Defending against the penalty corner as a
standard situation with the goalkeeper behind
the backs (defenders) (mini hockey). The
goalkeeper runs out just in front of the
goal – defenders (2 and 4) stay in the goal
mouth to cover it – defender (3) runs at the
striker – defender (1 and 5) run at the attacker
as in the illustration. In outdoor hockey no
more than five defenders may stand behind
the goal or dead ball line; the remaining
players stand beyond the centre line.

3/5

6. Penalty corner – Defence

Defending against the penalty corner as a
standard situation with the goalkeeper in

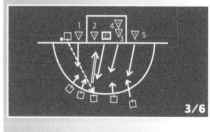

3/6

front of the backs (defenders) (mini hockey hockey). The goalkeeper runs out at the striker – defenders (2 and 4) stay behind in the goal mouth to cover it – defenders (1,3 and 5) run as a 'second wave' at the attackers as in the illustration. [Defenders – see Number 5].

A

4. Description of the movements

a) Penalty corner – Defence
Goalkeeper behind the back defenders
(Indoor hockey)

1. All the players stand on the opposite side of the goal from where the penalty corner is being taken.
2. All the defenders stand holding their sticks behind the dead ball line in two rows.
3. The quickest defender stands next to the goal post and runs at the striker.
4. The remainder run to take position as agreed beforehand in order to cover and mark the goal mouth and defend against attacking variations or a rapid counter-attack (see sketches on pages 147 and 148).

B

b) Goalkeeper in front of the back defenders (Indoor hockey)

1. All the players stand on the opposite side of the goal from where the penalty corner is being taken.
2. All the defenders stand holding their sticks behind the dead ball line in two rows.
3. The goalkeeper runs at the striker in order to save with his body.
4. The remainder run to take position as agreed beforehand (See sketch on Page 148).
5. The players in the rear row cover the goal mouth.

149

c) Goalkeeper behind the back defenders (Outdoor hockey full and mini hockey pitch)

1. No more than five (full pitch) or six (mini hockey) players on the defending side may defend against the corner; the remainder of the players have to stand behind the centre line.

2. The five (or six) players stand holding their sticks behind the goal line, in the goal mouth or behind the goal line on both sides of the goal, but at least 4.55m away from the penalty corner taker.

3. Two (full pitch) or three (mini hockey) players stand first of all behind the goal line inside the goal mouth.

4. The goalkeeper runs just a little out away from the goal.

5. The quickest defender, who is standing next to the goal post nearest to where the penalty is being taken, runs at the striker.

6. The remaining players run to the previously agreed positions; no second row wave is possible.

d) Goalkeeper in front of the back defenders (Outdoor hockey)

1. No more than five (full pitch) or six (mini hockey) players on the defending side may defend against the corner; the remainder of the players have to stand behind the centre line.

2. The remaining five (or six) players stand holding their sticks behind the goal line, in the goal mouth or behind the goal line on both sides of the goal, but at least 4.55 m away from the penalty corner taker.

3. Two (full pitch) or three (mini hockey) players stand first of all behind the goal

line inside the goal mouth.

4. Two players stay to cover the goal from the goal line.

5. The remaining defenders run in a second wave to pre-determined positions in case the goalie is outmanoeuvred.

5. Incorrect movements

Penalty corner – defence

1. The quickest defender doesn't run at the striker (in the case of the goalkeeper behind the backs).

2. The goalkeeper doesn't run fast enough at the striker (in the case of the goalie in front of the backs); the fastest players follow him.

3. The players in the second row do not form proper cover in the goal. (I).

4. The goal is not defended at all (FP/MH).

5. A counter-attack is not launched.

6. Corrective measures

Penalty corner – defence

1. Place the quickest player next to the goal post farthest away from the penalty corner taker (I), or at the nearest goal post to the penalty corner taker (FP/MH).

2. The goalkeeper has to rush forward directly the penalty corner is taken; the remaining players follow him in order to prevent a shot at goal being made should the goalkeeper be outplayed.

3. The players in the second row run to take up covering the narrow and long corners of the goal mouth.

4. Place two (FP) or three (MH) players in the goal mouth before the penalty corner is taken (FP/MH).

5. Defend against the penalty corner in an offensive manner so you can build up your own game and exploit the advantage.

7. The rules

1. The penalty corner is considered ended when a goal is scored, or when the ball goes out over the goal line, or if the ball leaves the shooting circle at any point outside the goal mouth, or when the attacker causes an infringement, or when a penalty stroke is awarded against you in the defence. (FP/MH/I).

8. Tips

Penalty corner – defence

The umpire does not blow his whistle to allow the penalty corner to be taken. The defenders can only move when the ball is played. If the defenders run into the shooting circle, or cross over the centre line too early, the corner is taken again. The umpire should only let the penalty be retaken if the attackers would not be disadvantaged. If the attackers are in a favourable shooting position he should let the game continue. If the defenders run out too early for a second time during a penalty corner, the umpire should show the green card and indicate to the penalty flick spot as a warning. If a player on the same side runs too early during a corner he should stop the game for a penalty flick stroke.

Photo & Illustration Credits

Coverphoto: Bongarts Sportfotografie GmbH, Hamburg
Cover design: Birgit Engelen, Stolberg
Illustrations: Josef Marx, Düsseldorf and Tanja Dohr, Aachen
Photos: Horst Mevißen, Krefeld and Josef Marx, Düsseldorf

Index

Afternote

This book was written to give teachers and trainers a practical introduction to the teaching of hockey in schools and sports clubs. It has been designed, in a compact form, containing games and training exercises, a section on gymnastics, and covering techniques and tactics as well as points regarding the rules and playing tips, to make the daily work of training easier.

The great deal of positive feedback that we have received on earlier editions (written in the German language), has shown us that the book has been universally accepted, mainly because of the concept of playing the game – "one plays hockey right from the word 'Go!" – and this has been the main way it has been used.

For us, the knowledge that it has been used so much in this way, is praise and recognition enough.

Our thanks goes to Mr Hans Braun of the School for Fitness and Spinal Exercises at the Health Park, Krefeld for his help in providing advice for the re-working of the gymnastics exercises, as well as to Mr Ralph Bonz, Rheinbek, Member of the Commission of Umpires of the DHB (German Hockey Association) for the updating of the hockey rules.

Josef Marx   *Günter Wagner*

The Authors

Josef Marx

- Studied in Neuss and Düsseldorf
- Has taught in Secondary Modern and High Schools since 1968
- Has held the lectureship for Hockey education at the Heinrich-Heine University Düsseldorf since 1982

Günter Wagner

- Studied in Neuss
- Has taught in different types of school since 1974
- The main teaching emphasis of his physical education work in Krefeld is Hockey

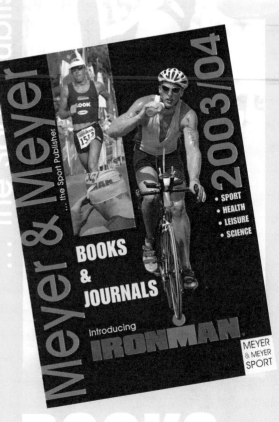

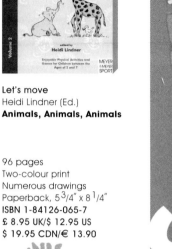

Let's move
Heidi Lindner (Ed.)
**Great Games
for Small Children**

96 pages
Two-colour print
Numerous drawings
Paperback, $5^3/4'' \times 8^1/4''$
ISBN 1-84126-064-9
£ 8.95 UK/$ 12.95 US
$ 19.95 CDN/€ 13.90

Let's move
Heidi Lindner (Ed.)
Animals, Animals, Animals

96 pages
Two-colour print
Numerous drawings
Paperback, $5^3/4'' \times 8^1/4''$
ISBN 1-84126-065-7
£ 8.95 UK/$ 12.95 US
$ 19.95 CDN/€ 13.90

Let's move
Heidi Lindner (Ed.)
Off we go outside!

96 pages
Two-colour print
Numerous drawings
Paperback, $5^3/4'' \times 8^1/4''$
ISBN 1-84126-066-5
£ 8.95 UK/$ 12.95 US
$ 19.95 CDN/€ 13.90

Let's move
Heidi Lindner (Ed.)
Wintertime

96 pages
Two-colour print
Numerous drawings
Paperback, $5^3/4'' \times 8^1/4''$
ISBN 1-84126-067-3
£ 8.95 UK/$ 12.95 US
$ 19.95 CDN/€ 13.90

MEYER & MEYER Sport | Von-Coels-Straße 390 | D-52080 Aachen | Fax +49 (0)2 41- 9 58 10-10